Twayne's United States Authors Series

Sylvia E. Bowman, *Editor*

INDIANA UNIVERSITY

James Fenimore Cooper

 II

JAMES FENIMORE COOPER

by DONALD A. RINGE

TWAYNE PUBLISHERS
A DIVISION OF G. K. HALL & CO., BOSTON

FOR LUCY

Contents

Chapter

Chronology   11

1.   Beginnings   17

2.   The American Past   26

3.   Europe and the United States   56

4.   Values in Conflict   91

5.   The Decay of Principle   115

6.   A General Estimate   145

Notes and References   157

Selected Bibliography   165

Index   172

About the Author

With degrees from Tulane and Harvard, DONALD A. RINGE has taught at Tulane and, since 1953, at the University of Michigan, where he is an associate professor of English. His field of special interest is American literature of the early nineteenth century, most particularly the interrelation of literature and fine art during the time of Bryant, Irving, and Cooper. He has published a number of articles in, among others, *PMLA, American Literature, American Quarterly, New England Quarterly, Nineteenth-Century Fiction,* and *College Art Journal.*

These articles have generally fallen into one of three groups. A number have been concerned with the intellectual milieu of William Cullen Bryant, his interest in science, his criticism of the fine arts, and his intellectual and artistic relations with such painters as Thomas Cole and such poets as Walt Whitman. A group has been concerned also with Cooper's artistic affinities with Thomas Cole, and with the interpretation and criticism of Cooper's late novels. A third has dealt more specifically with the artists themselves, the aesthetic theory of the Hudson River Painters and the philosophic background of functionalist theory.

Preface

THIS BOOK intends quite frankly to state the case for James Fenimore Cooper. It agrees with Marius Bewley that Cooper has long been undervalued as an artist, and with Charles A. Brady that his case should be reopened and judged once again. Thus, although it recognizes his well-known faults and failures, it chooses not to emphasize them, but to stress instead the thematic interpretation of his tales and the means, sometimes highly successful, by which he gave his themes expression. It asks the reader, therefore, to lay aside his preconceptions, to see the novels in their own terms, and to seek the meaning that they, like all works of literary art, will yield if carefully read for themselves alone. The purpose is to understand the tales that they may be evaluated in the light of that knowledge.

For this reason, I have severely limited the amount of biographical and historical information contained in this book. I have included only that which is necessary for continuity and for an understanding · of the background and subject matter of particular novels. It is the tales themselves that are important today, if Cooper is to be studied at all; and I do not want to interpose too much material between the reader and the direct perception of Cooper's art. The space devoted to particular tales has been deliberately apportioned to draw attention to many of Cooper's late novels which deserve to be better known, and which must figure at least as largely as his early work in any just evaluation of his achievement.

Several of the conclusions presented here I have already expressed in completely different form in *PMLA, American Literature, Nineteenth-Century Fiction,* and *Papers of the Michigan Academy of Science, Arts, and Letters.* For permission to rework some of the material used in these articles, I am grateful to the editors of the aforementioned journals, to The Regents of the University of California, and to Mr. Fred Wieck, Director of the University of Michigan Press.

Many of the debts I have incurred in my study of Cooper can never be completely acknowledged, for they are owed to all the scholars who have preceded me in the field. To Professor Howard Mumford Jones, however, who first introduced me to Cooper the *moraliste*, I owe a particular debt of many years' standing for his guidance and encouragement of my work on Cooper and his contemporaries. Finally, to my wife, I owe a special acknowledgment for her trenchant criticism of the manuscript and for her patient endurance of the many hours of silence while the work went on.

D. A. R.

Ann Arbor, Michigan
March, 1961

Chronology

1789   James Cooper (the "Fenimore" was added in 1826) born September 15 at Burlington, New Jersey.

1790   Family moved to Cooperstown, New York, in November.

1803-   Entered Yale College in February, 1803. Dismissed for
1805   misconduct in 1805.

1806-   Went to sea as common sailor on the *Stirling*, October,
1807   1806, to prepare for entering Navy. Visited England and Spain. Returned to America in September, 1807.

1808-   Commissioned midshipman in the Navy, January 1,
1811   1808. Served on the *Vesuvius*, was stationed at Oswego on Lake Ontario, and served under Lawrence on the *Wasp*. Resigned after three and a half years service, the last year of which was spent on furlough.

1811-   Married Susan Augusta DeLancey, January 1, 1811.
1820   To them were born five daughters and two sons. Settled in Westchester in 1817, after living at Mamaroneck and at Cooperstown. Built home at Angevine Farm near Scarsdale in 1818.

1820   Began literary career with *Precaution*.

1821-   The period of Cooper's greatest success, most of which
1826   was spent in New York City, and during which he published *The Spy* (1821), *The Pioneers* (1823), *The Pilot* (1824), *Lionel Lincoln* (1825), *The Last of the Mohicans* (1826).

1826-   Sailed for Europe with his family, June 1, 1826. Landed
1828   in England, then went to Paris in July, 1826, where he stayed until February, 1828. Published *The Prairie* (1827), *The Red Rover* (1827).

1828-   In London from March through May, 1828. Crossed to
1830   Low Countries and journeyed to Switzerland. In Oc-

tober, 1828, crossed Alps into Italy, where he stayed until May, 1830; visited Florence, Leghorn, Naples, Rome, Venice. Published *Notions of the Americans* (1828), *The Wept of Wish-ton-Wish* (1829).

1830-
1832
To Germany in May, 1830. The July Revolution recalled him to Paris in August, 1830, where he stayed until July, 1832. Friendship with Lafayette led him to take part in the Finance Controversy. Served on American Polish Committee to aid the Poles in their struggle for freedom. Published *The Water-Witch* (1830), *The Bravo* (1831).

1832-
1833
Revisited Belgium in July, 1832, and returned to Switzerland. In October, 1832, returned to Paris, where he stayed until the summer of 1833. Published *The Heidenmauer* (1832).

1833
Spent the summer in England and embarked for the United States, September 28. Refused public dinner in his honor. Published *The Headsman* (1833).

1834-
1836
Retired as novelist in *A Letter to His Countrymen* (1834), but continued to write satire and non-fiction. Settled finally in Cooperstown. Published *The Monikins* (1835), and five volumes of travels (1836-38).

1837
Controversy over Three Mile Point at Cooperstown, and the beginning of Cooper's war with the Whig press in July and August. In September began first of many suits for libel.

1838
Struggle with libelous press intensifies with publication of *Home as Found*, which, with *Homeward Bound*, marks his return to novel writing. Also published *The American Democrat*.

1839-
1843
War with the press continues, intensified by controversy over Cooper's account of the Battle of Lake Erie in his *Naval History* (1839). By 1843, most of the cases were settled. Meanwhile, Cooper returned to pure fiction with *The Pathfinder* (1840), *Mercedes of Castile* (1840), *The Deerslayer* (1841), *The Two Admirals* (1842), *The Wing-and-Wing* (1842), *Wyandotté* (1843).

1844- Came to the landlords' defense in the anti-rent agi-
1846   tation in New York State, and wrote the Littlepage
       novels (1845-46) to present his views. Published *Afloat
       and Ashore* (1844), *Miles Wallingford* (1844), *Satanstoe*
       (1845), *The Chainbearer* (1845), *The Redskins* (1846).

1847- Cooper's last years, during which his work took on an in-
1850   creasingly religious tone. Published *The Crater* (1847),
       Jack Tier (1848), *The Oak Openings* (1848), *The Sea
       Lions* (1849), *The Ways of the Hour* (1850).

1851   Died, September 14, at Cooperstown. leaving
       The Town of Manhattan unfinished.

James Fenimore Cooper

CHAPTER 1

Beginnings

WHEN JAMES FENIMORE COOPER published *Precaution* at the age of thirty-one, he was a gentleman farmer turned novelist by accident. Half of his life was already behind him, a life that had shown little promise of what was to come. Reared at Cooperstown, New York, a village well past the frontier stage, he had grown up the son of a wealthy land speculator, attended Yale until he was dismissed for a prank in his junior year, made a voyage to Europe in a merchant vessel, and served for several years in the Navy. After his marriage to Susan Augusta DeLancey, he settled down to a comfortable life which was typified by his membership in the local agricultural and Bible societies, his commission as colonel in the militia, and his investment in a whaling vessel. To all appearances, he was a landed gentleman who would spend his life in such mundane activities. On a dare from his wife, however, the man who did not like to write even a letter set out to compose a better book than the English one he had been reading to her.[1] Although it is doubtful that he won his bet with *Precaution*, he launched a career that was to end thirty-one years later only after the publication of some thirty-two novels and at least a dozen volumes of non-fiction.

I *The Problem*

It was truly a fortunate accident that turned Cooper into a writer, for the obscure New York gentleman embarked on a course that was to place him first in the line of major American novelists. To be sure, Cooper is not usually accorded so high a position in American fiction; for, although he has always had his defenders, his reputation by and large has steadily declined for over a century. Cooper has been, in Marius Bewley's words, so "consistently underestimated as an artist"[2] that today his work is widely regarded as hardly fare for mature readers. His tales of the forest and sea have been relegated to the rank of children's books and the rest of his novels are left unread on the shelves of libraries. Many literate Americans know him only through Mark Twain's delightfully funny but grossly unfair criticism;[3] and, assuming that Twain is giving a just account of *The Deerslayer,* they fail to read even the best of Cooper's novels. Indeed, so low has Cooper's reputation fallen that at least one reviewer of an excellent study by Charles A. Brady has expressed some surprise at the treatment that Brady accords him.[4]

But Cooper has not been entirely neglected. Several excellent biographies have already been written,[5] and the standard histories of American literature generally give him his due. His historical importance is unquestioned. As Howard Mumford Jones has shown, the number of "firsts" to be attributed to Cooper is truly astonishing. He created the modern tale of the sea and was the first to make effective use of the frontier. He wrote as well the first American Utopia and the first American novels to describe the lives of succeeding generations of characters.[6] Among his first four books are two truly revolutionary ones, *The Pioneers* and *The Pilot;* and in *The Last of the Mohicans* he composed what is perhaps the classic tale of frontier adventure. Too much stress on this aspect of Cooper's work, however, has had an unfortunate consequence: it has drawn perhaps too much attention to Cooper's early tales to the detriment of his later, more sophisticated ones. More people know *The Spy* than *The Bravo* or *Wyandotté, The Last of the Mohicans* than *The Deerslayer, The Pilot* than *The Two Admirals* or *Afloat and Ashore.* Ironically, Cooper is best known for what is essentially his apprentice work. Except for the Littlepage series, the late novels are all but unknown to the non-specialist, yet they include some of his most vigorous books.

Too much attention to Cooper's historical importance has also had another unfortunate effect. Through the excellent work of Robert E. Spiller and others, we have come to a clear understanding of Cooper's social and political thought. We know that he critically observed the manners and morals of Europe during his seven-year tour of England and the Continent; we also know that on his return to America he not only continued to be what he had always been, a staunch defender of American principles, but became as well a caustic critic of American practice. His lover's quarrel with his country, his war with his fellow citizens and with the press, his innumerable and involved libel suits—all are important elements in Cooper's biography. But undue stress upon them directs attention to some of Cooper's weakest novels. Books like *Homeward Bound* and *Home as Found* are of the utmost importance in the study of Cooper's intellectual development and must always be accorded their due proportion of space in any consideration of Cooper's achievement, but they add relatively little to our understanding of his artistry. Besides, although Spiller was always careful to indicate that Cooper the social critic was not the whole man, so well did he do his work that today the tendency is to think of Cooper as primarily a critic of his times.

Thus, the reader of Cooper's fiction who limits himself to a few of the early tales and to perhaps a volume of his social criticism is apt to come away with several mistaken notions. He is likely to see in Cooper's work a dichotomy between his tales of adventure and romance and his novels of social purpose. Certainly, *The Last of the Mohicans* would seem at first glance to have little thematic connection with *Home as Found,* and the reader who samples the tales in this way is left with the impression that Cooper's fiction is diverse and disunified. He is also likely to conclude that Cooper was unable to draw believable well-born characters. To be sure, one can hardly defend a large number of his ladies and gentlemen. From Harper in *The Spy* to Edward Effingham in the "Home" novels, from the Munro sisters in *The Last of the Mohicans* to Eve Effingham, Edward's daughter, most of them are stiff and unconvincing. Less well understood, however, is that beginning with *The Pathfinder* Cooper draws few such socially élite characters, and those he does present, like Miles Wallingford and the Littlepage heroes, are very well done.

Indeed, Cooper's women, for whom he has been frequently criticized, are weak mainly in the early volumes.[7] Judith Hutter in *The Deerslayer*, Lucy Hardinge in the Wallingford novels, and Anneke Mordaunt in *Satanstoe* are convincingly drawn.

We should not minimize Cooper's real and annoying faults. We may justly criticize the use he makes of stock situations in plotting his novels, like the return of the lost heir in *The Pioneers,* or the disguised and mysterious gentleman who turns out to be John Effingham's son in the "Home" novels. Cooper took from contemporary fiction whatever might be useful to his own purposes and is frequently guilty of triteness in his plotting. His style, moreover, is often defective, especially when he tends to prolixity and Latinate phrasing. But neither of these faults is really so serious as much of the criticism seemingly implies. As Yvor Winters has shown, Cooper could sometimes write extremely well,[8] and the worst that can be said of much of his writing is that it is so very old-fashioned. He frequently wrote too much and too rapidly, but once we become accustomed to his mode of expression, the style can be accepted with all its faults as an adequate vehicle for what he is trying to do. It served very well to detail the recurring patterns of action that dominate most of his books, and it was especially suitable for the descriptions of physical nature that affect to so great an extent the ultimate meanings in his novels.

II *Intrinsic Values*

For Cooper's strength rests not in style nor in the psychological probing of character. He is neither a Hawthorne nor a Henry James. His special gifts lay in narrative and description, through both of which, as several perceptive critics have discerned, he communicates his fundamental themes. In Cooper, the description of nature was never just an adjunct to his tale, nor merely a framework for the action. As Joseph Conrad observed over sixty years ago, nature for Cooper was always an essential factor in the problem of existence. For all the majestic sweep of his vast seascapes, the sea so interpenetrates with life that it ever remains in touch with the men who "traverse its immense solitudes" in pursuit of war or gain.[9] Conrad pays tribute both to the faithfulness of Cooper's depiction of the sea and the use he made of it as an important factor in the action itself. It was not just the sea, however, that Cooper could draw to the life. His descriptions of the American forests, of the Great Lakes, and of the High Plains have the same essential truth; and they function in a similar way in his tales.

In depicting man's relation to his natural environment, Cooper expressed a "great religious vision of life," which, as Howard Mumford Jones has shown, he shared with many of his contemporaries in both literature and the fine arts.[10] Through his descriptions of the majestic order of the natural landscape, he was able to present both the principle of divine harmony everywhere apparent in the physical world and the need for humility in men who are dwarfed by the immensity of the God revealed in nature. Cooper was always a deeply religious man. Although for most of his life he was not a communicant in a specific church, he always affirmed the fundamental values of religious belief; and his works, both early and late, have a strong moral tone. As time wore on, his themes took on a more specifically Christian coloration, for in his later years he became increasingly attached to the Episcopal Church. As Grossman has shown in *James Fenimore Cooper,* he served both as warden in the local parish and as a "delegate to Episcopal diocesan conventions in New York" long before he was finally confirmed by his brother-in-law, Bishop DeLancey, in the last months of his life (pp. 254-55). But we need not point to his final conversion for evidence of Cooper's fundamentally moral view. From the very beginning, Cooper had shown through his picture of man in relation to the immensity of physical nature the importance of the religious view of life both for the individual himself and for the proper ordering of society.

We must always take into account, therefore, the interrelation of man and nature in Cooper's work. To do otherwise is to court the serious danger of misunderstanding completely the fundamental meaning that Cooper is trying to express; for, beginning with *The Spy,* the physical setting both defines the problem in, and sets the moral tone for, many of his tales. Nor can we afford to dismiss the narrative parts of Cooper's books as pure adventure—as action which is its own excuse for being. To be sure, Cooper's narrative skill is great, both in the well-paced movement of entire novels, like *The Last of the Mohicans,* and parts of novels, like the night ride on the thawing river in *Satanstoe.* But this action does not exist for itself alone; and we have come recently to understand the thematic use that Cooper made of characters in action and to see the relation of the material to the over-all meaning of the tales. Marius Bewley in *The Eccentric Design* has shown the moral significance of "action as a phenomenon of the physical world" in Cooper's best work (pp. 73-74), and demonstrates in his admirable analysis of *The Deerslayer,* how Deerslayer's values exist not as a "separable commentary on the action" but lie "in the heart of the action itself" (p. 89). The narrative mode must thus be considered an integral part of Cooper's art.

When Cooper's work is seen in these terms, it becomes apparent, as Brady has argued, that the case for Cooper should be reopened, that he should be "revalued as something much more than a pioneer novelist who is extrinsically important because he happens to have been first in certain fields" (p. 59). Historically significant though he may be, Cooper deserves consideration for the intrinsic value of his work. His work, of course, is uneven, for he sometimes became so concerned with the ideas he was developing, as in some of the social criticism of the 1830's and 1840's, that he all but ignored the artistry of their expression; and the novels, intellectually vigorous though they certainly are, can scarcely be called works of art. But at his best, Cooper is a serious artist who could generate an important moral theme from the skillful handling of his material. In his better work—and this bulks much larger than many suppose—Cooper was able to express his moral view of man in terms of convincing characters acting in a believable world. These are truly works of lasting significance, novels that can be read today both for the validity of their themes and the artistry of their expression.

Cooper, of course, did not find at once his best techniques, nor was he entirely consistent in their development. Never a theorizer about aesthetic questions, he plunged into his career without preparation and learned his craft as he practiced it. He was perfectly capable, therefore, of writing a thoroughly wretched book, like *Lionel Lincoln,* immediately after one of his most successful ones; and he could sometimes abandon his fine techniques of narrative and description to write so dull and wordy a tale as *Mercedes of Castile.* By and large, however, Cooper's talent developed as he practiced his art; and the general movement of his work is forward to more complex themes and increasing skill in developing them.

Although in his later work he sacrificed to some extent the exciting action of his earlier tales, he more than made up for the loss by his skillful handling of the much more sophisticated themes. But Cooper's development did not entail any basic change in his point of view. Seen as a whole, his work is remarkably unified in the rather sweeping moral vision of life that appears in all of his tales both early and late. What Cooper did throughout his career was to refine his ideas about God, man, and society in the light of his increasing experience; to express different elements of his view at different times; and eventually, in his best work, to unite the major streams of his thought into the well-planned books that artistically express his ideas.

III *Precaution*

Cooper's apprentice novel, however, showed no such promise, and most critics have been only too happy to dismiss it at once and to discuss his better work. In a sense they are right. *Precaution* (1820) is indefensible, and no one would recommend it to the general reader. Yet the book is not without its value. We can sometimes learn much from an artist's failure, especially if it is with an early work. We can at least discern the ideas that initially interested him and observe the means, however fumbling, by which he strove to give them expression. Regarded in these terms, *Precaution* is of some importance in contributing to our understanding of Cooper's art.

In this complicated story of domestic manners imitative of the school of Jane Austen, the central issue is the care parents should take to insure the proper marriage of their daughters. In his treatment of this problem, Cooper clearly reveals his early interest in social themes and his insistence upon the application of moral principle as a guide to action. The lack of true principle in the Moseleys' guidance of their daughters leads to Jane's deeply felt hurt when Colonel Egerton, the man she loves, runs off with another girl who has just inherited a fortune. On the other hand, the adherence to principle on Emily's part is ultimately rewarded by her marriage to the rich and generous Lord Pendennyss. Despite its sentimental nonsense, the novel does reveal Cooper's first gropings toward the affirmation of principle that was to become an important element in his maturest novels.

More significant, however, in view of his later work, is Cooper's concern with the problem all men face in penetrating the appearance of things to the truth that lies behind it. This theme is expressed in *Precaution* in a number of ways. Part of the problem that Jane Moseley faces is her need to discern the truth of the Colonel's character through the very pleasant appearance he presents in society; Emily confronts the opposite problem of perceiving George Denbigh's true character when all appearance is against him. Even one of the minor elements in the book adds to the development of this theme; for Mr. Benfield, who has preserved his dream of the beauty and faith of Lady Juliana for forty years, comes face to face with the horrible reality of what she truly is and his illusion is forever destroyed (p. 385). This contrast of appearance and reality recurs again in Cooper's work as soon as *The Spy* and as late as *The Ways of the Hour*. In every instance, he seeks a reliable means for discerning the truth; and he always returns to religious principles, applied in *Precaution* by Mrs. Wilson, Emily's guide, as the proper basis for judgment. Cooper began, therefore, in his first novel to develop some of his most important moral concepts.

But if the theme in *Precaution* dimly foreshadows what is to come, the form does not. The lifeless characters moving like cardboard figures through an unreal world are not what we expect from Cooper, nor are the paucity of action and the almost total absence of physical description. We discover none of the dense reality of the physical world that we find in his subsequent novels, none of the accurate depiction of characters in action that he later learned to handle so well. Both characters and incidents are manipulated to achieve the desired end; they serve to illustrate the theme rather than actually to generate it. We miss here, too, the well-developed actions typical of Cooper at his best. Instead, we find a complicated tale in which characters crowd upon characters, and incident rapidly follows incident, until the story itself breaks down completely, and Cooper has to devote endless pages to retrospective narrative late in the book to untangle the various relations.

Part of Cooper's failure in *Precaution* surely resulted from his attempt to pass it off as the work of an Englishman, a deception which he practiced for fear that an American work would not be well received. Because Cooper deliberately attempted to describe a kind of life that he knew only from books, his novel everywhere reveals its unsubstantial foundation. Most of his failure derived, however, from his own inexperience. Like all beginning writers, he had not yet learned to exploit his materials; therefore, his incidents are sketchily drawn and poorly developed. Yet for all his mistakes in *Precaution*, Cooper knew what he should be doing. The care with which he tries to present parallel and contrasting variations upon the central theme of the conflict of appearance and reality certainly shows that, even in his initial effort, Cooper perceived the means by which a novel should present its meaning and made the attempt, though unsuccessfully, to express the theme in this way.

Precaution is clearly the work of an intelligent amateur who knew what a book should do, but who could not yet succeed in making it come out right. That he failed is relatively unimportant. He had learned from his experience that he could sustain a full-length novel—and do it sufficiently well to justify his making a second attempt at fiction.

CHAPTER 2

The American Past

ALTHOUGH Cooper's apprentice novel was a rather dismal failure, it did get him fairly started on his career and opened the way for the much superior work that followed. Before *Precaution* was through the press, Cooper was already at work on *The Spy*, an "American novel professedly," which he early recognized as "far better than 'Precaution'."[1] Although Cooper was not always so enthusiastic about his second book during its composition—for several months he stopped work on it completely—he brought it to a successful if somewhat abrupt conclusion and published it in December, 1821.[2]

With the publication of *The Spy*, Cooper's career was firmly launched. By turning to the American scene, he had found material for a novel that became both a popular and an artistic success; and, if he still had doubts about the willingness of the American public to read books about native subjects, the great success of *The Pioneers* some thirteen months later must surely have removed them. For during the next few years or until 1831, he was to develop his themes exclusively through the use of native American materials in a series of nine books. Among them are *The Spy, The Pilot*, and the first three Leatherstocking tales upon which much of his reputation still depends.

I *Associationist Psychology*

Cooper was not reflecting a narrow nationalism in his choice of subjects; for, although this was a period of strong nationalistic feeling following the War of 1812, Cooper himself, though always loyal to American principles, was never an unreasoning chauvinist. Actually, his choice of material was probably the result of other considerations, most particularly the associationist psychology that underlay the aesthetic opinion of the times. To Cooper's contemporaries, the greatest value of a work of art lay in its suggestiveness, in its ability to arouse a suitable train of associations in the mind of the reader and to impart to him some fundamental truth. This process would obviously be most fruitful when both author and reader were well acquainted with the material used to express the theme, and the theme would most likely be true if it were based upon direct observation and knowledge. For this reason, poets, novelists, and painters turned to native materials to express their themes; and the first flowering of American art resulted.

Yet the very theory that led American artists to native subjects also induced doubts about their usefulness. There was the danger that the native materials might be too commonplace to be truly suggestive. Cooper reflects this belief in the third preface he wrote for *The Spy* in 1822: American subjects are so familiar to native readers and the democratic way of life has so tended to narrow the extremes of manners to a central average as to pose a serious problem to the writer of fiction.[3] In *Notions of the Americans,* he develops the concept at even greater length, concluding that, although the prevailing common sense of American life may be both "useful and respectable" in practical affairs, it provides few materials for the serious artist.[4] In his choice of native subjects, then, Cooper, like other writers and painters in his generation, faced a serious artistic problem. He had to use material through which he could make his fundamental beliefs completely intelligible to his readers. At the same time he had to find the means for creating the suggestiveness the aesthetic theory demanded. At times he failed, as in the Gothic absurdities of *Lionel Lincoln* and the bizarre supernaturalism of *The Water-Witch.* In his first three "American" books— *The Spy, The Pioneers,* and *The Pilot*—he found, however, material that served his purpose extremely well.

The neutral ground above New York during the Revolution in *The Spy,* Cooperstown of a generation before in *The Pioneers,* and the sea in *The Pilot*—each not only provided a densely realistic background for the development of his themes but enabled him to arouse suitable associations in the minds of his American readers. The exploits of Washington's army in Westchester County and the daring raid of John Paul Jones on the British coast were certain to appeal to the patriotism of his audience, and the description of the new settlement in *The Pioneers* was sure to suggest the westward march of American civilization. Besides such obvious materials, however, Cooper includes other elements that increase the suggestive quality of his tales. In all three books, he introduces characters who are far removed from the commonplace realities of American life. Harvey Birch, Leatherstocking, and Long Tom Coffin—all three highly individualized, asocial, and deeply religious men—represent a point of view in each tale that is far from the norm and that affirms a sense of values not always found in average national life. Birch's patriotism, Natty Bumppo's devotion to his friends and deep respect for the wilderness, and Coffin's love for the sea and obedience to his natural superiors help raise the books above the level of simple narrative and aid in the development of the central theme that Cooper presents in each.

II *Neutral Ground: The Spy*

Equally important in the development of his themes is the physical setting in which the characters move. Too little has been written of Cooper's sure sense of the physical landscape and the use he makes of it at times to create the fundamental issue in his books. The neutral ground in *The Spy*, like the forest or the Great Plains in the Leatherstocking tales and the sea in *The Pilot*, defines the problem that the characters face in resolving their conflicting interests. A physical and moral no-man's-land, it reflects the ambiguities that pervade the entire novel[5]—just as the forest in *The Pioneers* defines the conflict between Judge Temple and Leatherstocking and suggests the moral issue involved. So too does the Pilot's guidance of the American ship through dangerous shoals off the coast of England suggest the theme of the need for obedience to proper authority that lies at the heart of the book. In all three, the setting is of prime importance in suggesting the moral problems that the characters must solve.

In *The Spy* (1821), the physical environment defines the central conflict and sets the moral and ethical tone that dominates the book. The neutral ground between the British and American outposts is a moral wasteland where conflicting principles are at war and the only law is might. As Cooper writes in the opening chapter of the novel, "the law was momentarily extinct in that particular district, and justice was administered subject to the bias of personal interests, and the passions of the strongest" (p. 13). In this area the British and American armies, agents of conflicting views of government, meet in honorable battle. Here too the Cow-boys and the Skinners, irregular partisans who often fight as much for personal gain as for any higher motive, range almost unrestricted. The Skinners, in particular, under the guise of American patriotism, seek every opportunity to profit materially from their activities, and their leader is even capable of shifting sides, as he does at the end of the book, in the hope of profiting from his move. The setting of the novel suggests a moral chaos given over to those who can use the absence of law and order to their own advantage.

Into this neutral area, the elder Mr. Wharton moves with his family. Urged by a "constitutional prudence that pleaded loudly in behalf of his worldly goods" (p. 29), Mr. Wharton, a loyal subject of King George, has transferred all his money into British funds. To protect his landed estate, however, which he fears the rebels might seize, he has left the protection of the British troops in New York and has taken up residence in his summer home, "The Locusts," where he assumes a mask of neutrality. Unable to decide between property and principle, he straddles the fence and tries to remain on good terms with both sides. The moral weakness of his stand leaves him at the mercy of all the forces that sweep across the neutral ground; brings his son, the British captain, into danger when he comes in disguise to visit him; and eventually causes the loss of his house to the marauding Skinners, who burn and loot it in the name of American patriotism. In his refusal to adhere to honest principle, Wharton brings almost complete disaster on himself and his family.

The ambiguity of the elder Wharton's position is only one

of many unclear and uncertain relations in the book. With all order and coherence lost, very little is what it appears to be. An example is the remarkable scene in the early pages of the novel when Captain Wharton, Harper, and Harvey Birch all appear together in the Wharton house during a violent storm. In his guarded conversations with the Whartons, Birch manages to convey military information to Harper while he appears to the others to be passing on idle gossip as he shows them his wares. Birch is, of course, the spy from whom the book takes its name, a pariah cursed and hated by most, believed by all to be a British agent, but, beneath his dual disguise, Washington's favorite spy. The British captain, far from his own lines, is apparently a stranger in his own house, and Harper is really the commander-in-chief of the American army. All appear to be something other than what they are; and their relations to one another, like their conversations, are full of concealed meanings.

The disparity between appearance and reality established in this scene is reflected in other characters and incidents. Sarah Wharton accepts the British Colonel Wellmere as a gentleman and almost weds him before she learns that he is an unprincipled scoundrel who is already married; Frances, her sister, breaks her troth to the American Major Dunwoodie because she suspects him, unjustly, of being improperly involved with Isabella Singleton. Wherever one turns, the appearance of things is deceptive. Frances' sincere attempts to help her brother, Henry, when he is being tried as a spy, serve only to strengthen the case against him, and Dunwoodie's conviction that Henry will not be saved comes just at the time when Harper is acting secretly to free him. Even the appearance of justice is turned upside down. As Grossman has pointed out, Henry's trial, although it proceeds according to correct legal forms, is grossly unjust, for it would condemn an innocent man to an ignominious death as a spy. On the other hand, the lynching of the leader of the Skinners by the Cow-boys, while strictly extra-legal, has a rather grim justice of its own in that it is so richly deserved (pp. 27-28).

But although *The Spy* presents a convincing picture of the moral confusion that results from a disrupted society, Cooper does not let the book end on such a note. Rather, he affirms a fundamental system of value in those who, despite the ambiguity of their environment, are willing to commit themselves unconditionally to a sincere and honest belief. If Mr. Wharton's central failing is his inability to sacrifice his worldly goods to what he believes is right, his son's main virtue is his commitment to the British cause, whatever the consequences might be. If the Skinners' great fault is their eagerness to use the cloak of patriotism to hide their material greed, Major Dunwoodie's strength lies in his adherence to duty; he delivers his prisoner, Henry, to his superiors for trial as a spy although doing so entails the risk of losing Frances, the girl he loves. Such devotion to principle has nothing to do with the relative merits of the British and American causes; for, although American patriotism is the highest value affirmed in the book, virtue may exist on either side of the conflict. Henry Wharton and Major Dunwoodie are equally praiseworthy in that they will not let close personal ties interfere with their sworn duties. Both go out of themselves in adhering to a system of value that transcends their individual desires; and, unlike Mr. Wharton and the Skinners, they let no selfish considerations stand in the way of what they know they should do.

The best example of positive value in the book, however, is Harvey Birch, the double agent. As a spy, one whose true motives must always be concealed, he shares the ambiguity that pervades the neutral ground where he lives. He is superior to the other inhabitants, however, in that he seeks no personal gain from the war—indeed, he loses all his possessions to the greedy Skinners. He is even morally superior to the other sincere characters, for he has not their reward of public approval of his actions. He must be content with the knowledge that he is furthering the cause he adheres to and that he has the approval of the one man, Harper, who knows the truth. In a sense, Birch is the inverse of the elder Wharton, Colonel Wellmere, and the Skinners. They conceal a corrupt reality beneath the appearance of virtue; he conceals his virtue beneath a seeming corruption and lives reviled and distrusted by all. Whereas they stand to gain materially as a result of their disguise, he loses all his possessions because of the false appearance he must maintain and eventually refuses all reward for his services. As a character, Birch is beautifully drawn, despite some occasional posturing. When seen crossing the neutral ground at night—every path and trail of which he knows intimately—his pack on his back and pursued by his enemies, he becomes, in Brady's words, "a mythopoeic emanation, almost, of the American landscape" (p. 72); and he foreshadows the even greater Leatherstocking, another committed man, whom Cooper created in his next novel. Birch lives a life of deep and sincere faith in God and asserts a value of self-discipline and self-sacrifice that transcends personality and helps him rise above the limitations of his background and environment.

Read in these terms, *The Spy* clearly illustrates Cooper's ability to generate a significant theme from the interplay of setting, characters, and action; for, although it has its share of Cooper's usual faults, they by no means obscure the book's great virtues. To its discredit, Cooper's language is sometimes faulty—perhaps never more so than it was in *The Spy* before the revision of 1831[6]—and the high-born characters, like Harper and the young heroes and heroines, are frequently wooden. The novel also has its share of such stock characters as the Smollettian Dr. Sitgreaves. On the credit side, however, it is a thrilling tale of adventure which also conveys an important theme. Its truth derives from the dense reality of the natural setting, the relation of the characters to that setting, and a physical action that also has a consistent moral significance. In *The Spy*, Cooper mastered a technique of composing novels that was to stand him in good stead throughout his career. Essentially, he had learned how to dramatize his ideas—to make them come alive through the action of his tale.

III *The Pioneers*

Cooper's next novel, *The Pioneers* (1823),[7] although markedly different in tone from *The Spy*, further illustrates his characteristic technique. Called "A Descriptive Tale" on its title page, *The Pioneers* draws its fundamental meaning from the description of the society it portrays and the relation of that society to the natural environment—the American wilderness that must be invaded and destroyed if civilization is to

spread across the continent. Setting the scene at Otsego
Lake (Cooperstown) in 1793-94, Cooper pictures a society
just past the frontier stage; the settlement is secure from
Indian attack and the leading citizen has begun to pay some
attention to the refinements of life. The gap between the
social classes, however, has not yet become so large as to set
him completely apart from the rest of the villagers; for, although there is some pretension among the common people,
all men can still meet together in the tavern without undue
restraint on Christmas Eve for a pleasant celebration. Indeed,
Cooper presents a kind of pastoral idyl; taking the reader
through the entire year from Christmas Eve to October,
he describes a series of rural pastimes, like a shooting match
for the turkey in the winter, or the night-fishing on the lake
in summer. He depicts the scenes with the balanced mixture
of realism and nostalgic longing that lend the book its dominant mood.

Yet it is neither the description itself nor the main plot
that reveals the true meaning of the novel. The return of the
lost heir, Oliver Effingham, to claim the inheritance that he
mistakenly believes Judge Temple has wrongfully appropri-
ated is obviously a stock element and may be dismissed as a
concession to the popular taste of the times. More important
is the secondary plot in the book: the conflict between Judge
Temple and Natty Bumppo, here called Leatherstocking.
This conflict arises naturally from the realities of the physical
environment, and it not only poses a true moral problem
for the judge but suggests also an important theme about
the westward march of American civilization. The land on
which Templeton, the judge's settlement, is built has been
occupied for some forty years by Leatherstocking, who still
maintains his cabin on a nearby mountain with his friend
John Mohegan. He had befriended Temple when the latter
had first come to survey his lands, and the judge out of
gratitude has allowed Leatherstocking to hunt on his estate.

Stated this simply, the relationship between the two men
would seem to be idyllic, as indeed it would be could time
stop and all further change in the landscape be halted. The
process that the judge begins, however, moves forward with
a force of its own; and, as Templeton develops, the judge

and his old friend come inevitably into conflict. The change that civilization brings to the wilderness marks the area where they must inevitably clash. When the story opens, much of the natural landscape is still untouched. Virgin forest stretches uncut all around the town, pigeons on their annual migrations darken the sky as they fly past by the millions, and fish can be drawn in untold numbers from the lake. But the first ominous note of change has already been sounded. The larger game—most particularly deer—are becoming scarce; the people are making inroads on the forests of sugar maples, which they cut and waste for firewood. Leatherstocking and his Indian friend observe the change and lament it, for the process entails a moral wrong that Leatherstocking cannot tolerate.

The hunter maintains a moral view of nature, and he regards the bounty around him as provided by a beneficent God for man's use. A man is justified, he believes, in using whatever part of nature he truly needs; but he is not free to destroy at will. When he sees the settlers drawing in their seines with hundreds of fish, most of which will be left to rot on the shore, he can only lament the folly of men who can be so lawless in their relation to their natural surroundings (p. 291); and he is completely disgusted by the wholesale destruction of wildlife and by the cutting of trees. That Leatherstocking is fundamentally right in his view is abundantly demonstrated by the numerous scenes of irrational destruction that Cooper includes in the novel. Billy Kirby, an expert axman who delights in cutting trees, urges the destruction of thousands of pigeons and shoots wildly into the flock in a frenzy of killing (p. 270); Richard Jones, the judge's cousin and sheriff, actually brings out a swivel gun and lines up his men to fire volleys into the cloud of birds that is passing overhead (pp. 268-74). Wherever we read in the novel, there are scenes of senseless destruction or of settlers laughing at the idea that game or wood should ever become scarce.

Judge Temple himself clearly sees that such destruction is morally wrong and he is certainly opposed to it. The problem he faces, however, is how to control the waste without curtailing the advance of civilization. The judge's re-

course is to civil law, the law of society, which he hopes
to bring into accord with the moral law that Leatherstocking
is following in his relations with nature. He is pleased to
see the state legislature establishing seasons for the taking
of game, and he hopes eventually to make it a crime to cut
trees wantonly (p. 174). He enforces the law for the protection of deer with unswerving rigidity, and he demands
that the forms of society be respected even though the
law be administered for selfish aims by unworthy officers.
Thus, when Leatherstocking kills a deer out of season and
resists arrest by Hiram Doolittle, who tries to use the law
to satisfy his curiosity about what is in Leatherstocking's
cabin, the judge insists that the law be rigidly enforced. Judge
Temple's position is made doubly difficult in that Leatherstocking has recently saved his daughter, Elizabeth, by shooting a mountain lion which was ready to attack her. But he
adheres to his decision. Leatherstocking is sentenced to the
stocks and publicly humiliated.

The judge's argument in defending his actions is a good
one. As he tells his daughter, "Society cannot exist without
wholesome restraints. Those restraints cannot be inflicted,
without security and respect to the persons of those who
administer them; and it would sound ill indeed to report,
that a judge had extended favor to a convicted criminal,
because he had saved the life of his child" (p. 421). The
judge's logic is unimpeachable if men must have discipline
imposed on them by external authority, and Marmaduke
Temple has seen enough of the men in his settlement to
recognize that most will act from selfish motives or be
influenced by their overpowering passions before they will
exert the kind of self-control that would make the laws of
society unnecessary.[8] That Leatherstocking can resist most
of the selfish impulses of men makes him only the exception
that proves the rule. From his long life in the wilderness,
he has learned his true relation to nature and has acquired
the humility he needs to discipline himself in the moral
code taught him by the Moravian missionaries. But there is no
reason to assume that all men will be able to perceive and
follow such a system of belief. Human experience, indeed,
seems to suggest just the opposite; most men react like

Richard Jones, Billy Kirby, or Hiram Doolittle when no longer restrained by civil law.

Society demands, therefore, that the just man be punished that justice may prevail. To be sure, there is strong irony in the fact that Leatherstocking is persecuted for killing one deer out of season when the people of Templeton have slaughtered and chopped with complete impunity merely because they violated no man-made law. But Cooper wastes no sentimental tears on Leatherstocking's fate; for, although the hunter is caught in a cycle of change over which he has no control, he plays a vital part in the process which is ultimately working for good. In the last lines of the novel, Cooper comments on the role that Leatherstocking plays in the American drama. Of his own free will he leaves the settlement and disappears into the woods. "He had gone far towards the setting sun,—the foremost in that band of pioneers who are opening the way for the march of the nation across the continent" (p. 505). The asocial man, free from restraint except for those moral imperatives that bind men in all times and places, flees the sometimes unjust restraints of a civilized society. But his flight does him no good; it merely begins the cycle anew and makes it all the easier for those social injunctions to catch up with him. He becomes, therefore, the inevitable herald of the civilization he most wants to avoid.

The end result of this process is, of course, the good society of Templeton; but it need not be bought, Cooper insists, at a price of the rape of the wilderness, the indiscriminate destruction of nature. Men like Richard Jones could learn from Leatherstocking to take the long view and conserve the bounty that has been lavished upon the American settler. If they do not do so—and these are implications that are not fully developed until later tales in the series—the nation itself must eventually suffer the judgment of an exhausted earth. It is in Judge Temple's view, therefore, that the best compromise is to be found. Clearly he is bringing the values of Christian civilization to the wilderness and laying the foundation for a good society. Although he is willing to sacrifice much of nature to social order, he recognizes the values that are being lost and tries to some extent to curb at least part of the wanton destruction. The judge is certainly superior to his cousin and the other wasteful settlers, none of whom can be trusted to discipline themselves as Leatherstocking has. And, indeed, he is superior to the hunter too in the social values that he always affirms. Judge Temple is, therefore, the first of Cooper's long series of Christian gentlemen on whom he placed his faith for the establishment and maintenance of the good life.

IV   *The Pilot*

In *The Pioneers,* therefore, as in *The Spy,* Cooper was able to develop a significant theme from the realistic materials of American life. In both books, serious moral and ethical questions are posed by the realities among which the characters move; in both, the themes center around the fundamental need for personal restraint under the guidance of sound moral principle. Cooper's third great success, *The Pilot* (1824), concerns similar problems, and Cooper develops the material in terms of an environment that he also knew extremely well—the sea. That Cooper wrote the novel in answer to Scott's *The Pirate* to show what a real sailor would write of ships and the sea is a story that Cooper himself told and that has been often repeated. More important, however, is the fact that Cooper early recognized the opportunities afforded the novelist by life afloat. Admittedly, he never exploited the material so well as did Melville and Conrad after him, for he never quite succeeded in making a ship at sea suggest the world at large as they did. Yet the problems of leadership and obedience naturally suggested by men at sea and the question of authority posed by the very nature of the captain's office clearly caught Cooper's imagination; *The Pilot,* the prototype of a whole new kind of fiction, was the result.

That the physical environment is again of the utmost importance in understanding *The Pilot* is easily demonstrated. The time is once more the Revolution; the place, the coast of England, where two American men-of-war are cruising in preparation for a raid on the island. The plan is to capture hostages to insure good treatment of American prisoners.

For such a dangerous mission to succeed, strict obedience to proper authority is absolutely necessary; and this concept is clearly symbolized in the opening chapters of the novel when the Pilot (John Paul Jones) takes the ships through dangerous shoal waters where only he can guide them and all the men from Captain Munson down strictly obey him. Yet these same men are the agents of a revolutionary government that not only has denied obedience to the authority of the king but is actually in open rebellion against him. This problem, posed in the opening chapters, is the central issue in the book which unites the diverse episodes on sea and land into one coherent whole. Cooper examines the question from many points of view, both British and American; observes the dangers inherent in each side; and provides an answer in terms of the fundamental principle of self-discipline that we are already familiar with from both *The Spy* and *The Pioneers.*

To the Englishman on shore, the American Revolution is—in the words of Colonel Howard, a Tory who has fled the colonies—an "accursed, unnatural, unholy rebellion" (p. 202), a "damning crime" that must soon "call down the just wrath of Heaven on the transgressors" (p. 127). Rebellion against the king is, in Colonel Howard's eyes, rebellion against God because it destroys the constituted order and must soon end in chaos and tyranny. To escape these evils, he has brought his wards, Cecilia Howard and Katherine Plowden, back from the colonies with him; and both of them have deferred to his wishes although they are in love with a pair of American officers, Captain Barnstable and Lieutenant Griffith, who are, of course, on the warships cruising the coast. The colonel also supports a protégé, Christopher Dillon, whom he hopes to make a judge in the subdued colonies and whom he trusts, although it is soon apparent to the reader that he is an unprincipled villain. The colonel demands obedience from his wards, and freely gives his loyalty to the king; but, despite his admirable consistency, he illustrates the dangers of unreasoning obedience. For in his adherence to his cause, he justifies the treachery of his favorite when Dillon breaks his gentleman's word while bearing a flag of truce from the Americans. Because the colonel's unreasoning obedience blinds

him to fundamental principle, he makes the mistake of allowing the end he seeks—defense of the crown—to justify ignoble
means: treachery to one's pledged word.

The Americans, on the other hand, argue less formalistically.
To them, obedience is a virtue only when the authority is
just and competent. As the Pilot tells young Griffith on one
occasion, he wears the republican livery only because the
Americans are fighting "in behalf of human nature. Were
your cause less holy, I would not shed the meanest drop
that flows in English veins to serve it" (pp. 241-42). The forms
of authority and obedience are hollow mockeries if the reality
behind them is unprincipled. This position too, of course, has
its dangers, for how can one be certain that he is not blinded
by his personal wishes or that the principle he follows is a
valid one. Just as Colonel Howard is led astray by his own
desires, so also are some of the American officers. Barnstable
and Griffith know that the girls are in the vicinity of the
planned raid; and, when Griffith goes ashore with the Pilot
and a detachment of marines, he plans to communicate with
them. By following his personal desires while the Pilot pursues more serious duty, Griffith succeeds in alarming the
countryside. The Pilot's plans for the raid are frustrated,
one of the ships is wrecked, and the men barely escape with
the captured Colonel Howard and his two wards after a running battle with several British warships.

If Colonel Howard's blind obedience to corrupt authority
justifies the American cause, Lieutenant Griffith's error in
allowing personal desires to interfere with duty justifies the
colonel's fear of rebellion. Cooper even illustrates this point
at the end of the book when Barnstable and Griffith almost
come to blows in a dispute over what each wants to do, and
the British colonel observes: "Behold . . . the natural consequences of this rebellion! It scatters discord in their ranks;
and, by its damnable levelling principles, destroys all distinction of rank among themselves; even these rash boys know
not where obedience is due!" (p. 393).

Although both young men finally submit to the authority
of the Pilot in their dispute, a telling point has been made.
For Cooper in *The Pilot* is struggling with a question that
was to haunt him for many years, and he foreshadows a

theme that was to become increasingly important in his fiction. Deeply committed to American democracy on the one hand but clearly recognizing the dangers inherent in unrestrained human beings on the other, Cooper faced a dilemma that he does not really solve. To be sure, the Pilot himself imposes order and extricates the characters from their difficulties. We can take him, in other words, as "the man who knows and can act," the man to whom obedience is due. But the twentieth century reader distrusts this solution; for, if such a man be twisted by his passions, he could easily introduce the tyrannical dictatorship that Colonel Howard foresees as the logical end of the rebellion (p. 149).

We do not mean, of course, that Cooper specifically intended this conclusion to be drawn, for the tone of the whole book is clearly patriotic. But he is so sound in his analysis of the problem that the danger is certainly implicit in his development of it. Cooper is, moreover, careful at least to indicate the controls that are necessary if man is to avoid the dangers of the overpowering passions. In *The Pilot*, as in *The Spy* and *The Pioneers*, Cooper includes a character who has developed the self-control and the devotion to something beyond himself that are necessary for a stable democracy. Long Tom Coffin, like Harvey Birch and Leatherstocking, is a man of humble origin who lives so close to nature that he almost becomes a part of the natural scene. He is not, of course, so successful as the previous characters in representing moral principle. Less central to the action than Birch or Leatherstocking, he is also less important in the thematic development of the book; but he clearly resembles them in character and function. All three are honest, devoted men, with sincere religious convictions. They provide a moral undercurrent that forms a thematic thread in each book and that serves as a kind of touchstone of principle against which the values of other characters can be tested. All are isolated, asocial men who are not directly involved in society. But all exhibit the deep humility and the self-discipline, derived from their religious view of life, that are clearly needed if any system of order is to be maintained after the more formal restraints of society have been removed. By the time he completed *The Pilot*, therefore, Cooper had found not only his characteristic materials and techniques but also the themes that were to dominate his work for nearly thirty years.

V *Lionel Lincoln*

Cooper, of course, was not always so successful in developing his themes derived from the realities of the American experience. For his next novel, *Lionel Lincoln* (1825), Cooper did much research in an attempt to make his account historically accurate, but the diverse elements in the book simply do not add up to a significant theme. The carefully drawn—and justly praised[9]—descriptions of the retreat from Concord and of the Battle of Bunker Hill are overbalanced by the Gothic terrors and darkly hinted mysteries that Cooper saw fit to add. For the first time, too, Cooper indulges his sense of the melodramatic and pictures the British soldiers during the siege of Boston as brutal villains, the Bostonians as forbearing saints. Lionel Lincoln himself, Boston-born but an officer in the British army, perceives the difference; but, although he is increasingly influenced by the contrast he sees, this thematic development amounts to nothing. In the final scenes, the novel reverses its own logic; for Lionel returns to England without a qualm when the British army is evacuated.

Even the plot lines fail to contribute much to the novel's meaning. There is no real thematic connection between Lincoln's family problems and the basic setting of the book— besieged Boston. They are treated like so many unrelated elements, either of which would not be much changed if the other did not exist, a major flaw which sets the book far below the preceding three in which idea and incident are closely welded together. Indeed, even the superficial connection between the war and Lincoln's personal life that Cooper does include fails to help very much. Old Ralph, the pious patriot who moves at will through the opposing lines, turns out to be Lionel's father; and Job, an idiot boy who is a violent American partisan, is eventually revealed as his half-brother. But when Cooper reveals as well that Ralph is a maniac escaped from his British keeper, the reader is left with the impression that the two most influential patriots in Boston were both insane.[10] Such a conclusion is, of course, far from Cooper's intention, but the melodramatic inversion that comes at the end destroys all the coherence that the book appeared to have.

To be sure, many critics have found praiseworthy elements in the novel; some have even pointed out qualities that remind one of Hawthorne or Dostoevski;[11] but all agree that it is an unsuccessful book. A total failure, *Lionel Lincoln* remains the only volume of a projected series of historical novels, "Legends of the Thirteen Republics," that Cooper soon abandoned.

VI *Return to Leatherstocking*

It was fortunate indeed that Cooper turned away from this plan, for instead he composed *The Last of the Mohicans* (1826) and *The Prairie* (1827), which are among his acknowledged masterpieces and in which he further developed the character of Leatherstocking, a mythic figure worth any number of such contrived tales as *Lionel Lincoln*. He returned, moreover, in both of these frontier stories to the kind of material that had proved so useful in his previous successes—the natural landscape and its relation to the men and women who move through it. In *The Last of the Mohicans*, we enter the untouched wilderness around Lake George during the campaign of 1757, when Leatherstocking, now called Hawkeye, is in his early prime; in *The Prairie*, we are on the Great Plains about 1805, when Leatherstocking, here called only "the trapper," is well past eighty. Both tales pick up the thematic pattern we have already observed in *The Pioneers*: the moral implications of the westward march of civilization which Leatherstocking initiates and which finally destroys him.

This theme is less apparent in *The Last of the Mohicans* than in the other Leatherstocking tales, and most critics have been content to dismiss the book as almost pure adventure with slight social import.[12] It is true, of course, that the tale says little explicitly about the problem; but when we come upon it from *The Pioneers*—and this is the way it should be approached—we can easily recognize its relation to the earlier novel if we consider the mode of development Cooper uses in each book. *The Pioneers,* fundamentally descriptive, is essentially spatial in its development. The tone of secure repose that dominates the tale suggests the relatively secure life that the settlers have achieved at Templeton now that they have pushed back the wilderness, driven off hunter and Indian, and achieved a degree of civilized life. The narrative mode of *The Last of the Mohicans,* on the other hand—the pattern of chase, escape, and battle—suggests the fundamental insecurity of the whites when they penetrate the virgin wilderness for the first time and become dependent upon the Indians—and the Indian-like Hawkeye—for survival.

In *The Last of the Mohicans* everything is dominated by the virgin forest. The moment Duncan Heyward leads the girls, Alice and Cora Munro, off the main road between Forts Edward and William Henry, he loses control over his environment and becomes an easy prey to the machinations of the evil Magua. From this point to the end of the novel, all the white characters, with the exception of Hawkeye, are at the mercy of the wilderness and its natural, red inhabitants. Even Montcalm and the victorious French cannot completely govern their Huron allies after the evacuation of the fort, and the French commander himself muses about the dangers of setting in motion a process which he cannot control (p. 215). In the massacre at Fort William Henry, the Indians clearly dominate the whites who have invaded their lands. Indeed, even the English characters who finally succeed in recovering the stolen Alice from the Hurons must rely upon their Indian friends, the Delawares, to escape from being totally destroyed by the wilderness they have penetrated. Without Chingachgook and Uncas, the capable Hawkeye himself could have done little.

Even the scale of events is determined by the untouched wilderness. Whole armies are swallowed up in the living mass of dense vegetation only to emerge as broken and scattered remnants (pp. 13, 17); and the entire struggle between the British and French troops, with their white loyalties to distant kings, seems trivial when viewed in relation to the immense forest that surrounds them. Cooper deliberately draws his landscape on an immense canvas; the vast panorama he pauses to describe when the little party

led by Hawkeye approaches the fort for the first time deliberately suggests the immensity of space that surrounds
the little fort they see below (pp. 177-78). The white men,
dwarfed by their hostile environment, are incapable of
handling it; for the civilized principles they import are of
little value here. Overconfident in himself from the very beginning, Duncan Heyward constantly makes errors in judgment until Hawkeye bluntly warns him: "If you judge of
Indian cunning by the rules you find in books, or by white
sagacity, they will lead you astray, if not to your death"
(p. 259). Indeed, the massacre at William Henry speaks elo-
quently of the irrelevance of the white man's code of honorable surrender in the depths of the forest.

Only Hawkeye, of all the whites, is competent to survive,
mainly because his experience in the woods has instilled in him
the humility he needs to understand the Indian and to interpret the white and red man to each other. Superstitious,
ignorant, and prejudiced though he may be—qualities critics
have tended to ignore in him—he perceives as no other white
character does his true relation to the immensity of the nature
that surrounds him; and his humility lets him see good even
in his enemies. He alone sees virtue and justice among the
Indians as well as among those of his own color; and, although he always remains true to his race and consistently
maintains the superiority of the Christian view, he doesn't
make the mistake of completely scorning the heathen. He is
willing to learn from them, and his knowledge wins him
survival. Yet if Hawkeye's balanced view enables him to
cope with his environment and save the other whites from
certain destruction, it also sets in motion the chain of events
that eventually leads to his degradation in *The Pioneers.*

For the whites, hunted and insecure as they are in this
tale of suspense and violence, have already taken the first
steps toward complete mastery of the continent. The great
tribe of the Delawares has been scattered by the settlers,
and their enlistment in the white man's struggle against the
Hurons foreshadows the eventual destruction of both. Magua
is certainly right in asking the Delaware chiefs why Huron
and Delaware should "brighten their tomahawks, and sharpen
their knives against each other? Are not the pale-faces thicker

than the swallows in the season of flowers?" (p. 364). This question, repeated by Mahtoree in terms of Sioux and Pawnee in *The Prairie* (p. 415), should, of course, provide a rallying point for the tribes. That it does not is most fortunate for the whites and makes possible the ultimate conquest of the continent in the name of Christian civilization. That it also involves the death of Uncas, son of Chingachgook and beloved foster-son of Hawkeye, is not foreseen by these companions of the woods any more than is their own ultimate degradation. Only Tamenund, in the last pages of the book, can foresee the inevitable: "The pale-faces are masters of the earth, and the time of the red-men has not yet come again" (p. 443).

The Prairie shows the end toward which events are tending and brings the series to its logical point of repose in the great death scene of the trapper in the final pages of the book. The weakest of the three early Leatherstocking tales on the plot level—the kidnaping of Inez and the transporting of her to the trans-Mississippi west are most implausible—*The Prairie* is probably the richest thematically and the most complex intellectually. The relation of man to nature introduced in the two earlier books is further developed in terms of the immensity of the treeless waste of the Great Plains; the rape of the wilderness is described in less equivocal terms than in *The Pioneers;* and the moral view of nature is reaffirmed in the eloquent speeches of the aged trapper. In addition, Cooper goes out of his way to assemble a group of characters who run the whole gamut of American life from the "semi-barbarous" squatter, Ishmael Bush, to the refined Inez and Middleton, with Paul Hover and Ellen Wade forming the intermediate stages.[13] Indeed, Cooper even includes a scientist, Dr. Obed Bat, who, although actually a caricature, must be taken seriously because he introduces a new attitude toward nature, one as much opposed to the old trapper's view as that of the lawless squatter.[14]

As in the previous books, the relation of man to nature is fundamental to the tale, but the landscape is described as even more vast and sublime so that the characters seem all but completely dwarfed and overpowered by the immensity of grass and sky that stretches in every direction. Cooper had never seen the plains. He relied on books to give him the sense of a scene he did not personally know, and the authenticity of his description has been questioned.[15] But authentic or not, the setting of *The Prairie* serves the perfect aesthetic function in the book. Unlike *The Pioneers, The Prairie* depicts a world that man cannot pretend to master, for it is completely beyond his control; and unlike *The Last of the Mohicans,* it presents a gaunt, bare, hostile nature that leaves man naked to the elements. It is clearly a harsher world than that of the two previous volumes in the series.

But in many ways, the book directly complements *The Last of the Mohicans* and completes the cycle begun in it— and sometimes in precisely the same terms. The process that began on the eastern seaboard with the dislocation of the Delawares and the settling of the forest wilderness now moves into its final phase. As in *The Last of the Mohicans,* there is little law but might; and, although many of the whites are now more capable of coping with their environment, fundamentally they must still play one Indian tribe against another to attain their ends. Cooper has been accused of "laziness" in paralleling Hard Heart and Mahtoree with Uncas and Magua,[16] yet the repetition may well have been intentional. If Pawnee against Sioux recapitulates Mohican against Huron, the lesson is unmistakable: only the whites can win. And when the honest Hard Heart refuses to listen to the treacherous Mahtoree, just as the Delawares had ignored Magua's similar plea, he, like them, will be rewarded for his virtue with the extinction of his people. Even the trapper, who always laments the grievous wrong done the red man, never realizes the part he himself plays in bringing about his friends' destruction when he opens the path for the exploiters who follow.

The exploiters in this book, however, are not the settlers of *The Pioneers* who are building homes in the wilderness but their advance guard: Ishmael Bush and his tribe of lawless squatters who admit no authority over themselves, who are anti-social wanderers whose function in the settling of the country is to skim "the cream from the face of the earth" and get "the very honey of nature" (p. 311). If the

trapper represents the natural man who ·has disciplined himself as a result of his moral view of nature and thereby
earned his right to freedom, Ishmael Bush is the more usual
type who has confused liberty with license, who takes the
law into his own hands—as witness his execution of his
brother-in-law, Abiram White—and who asserts his own
mighty ego as the sole basis for all he does. Completely
selfish, Bush and his tribe attack · the physical landscape
with their axes in much the same way as did the settlers
in Templeton, but without their justification of bringing civilization to the wilderness. In effect, they confirm the opinion
of Marmaduke Temple that civil law is necessary to keep
men in check, for the implication of *The Prairie* is strong that
men without civil law are more likely to resemble Ishmael
Bush than the trapper. The wasted earth they leave behind
them is testimony to their moral state.

A more sophisticated exploiter, but one equally ominous for
the future, is Dr. Obed Bat, the satirized physical scientist
who accompanies Bush and who is in his own way as egotistical as the squatter. In his assumption of the scientific
view toward nature, Dr. Bat believes that all knowledge and
power will one day be within the reach of "reasoning, learned,
scientific, triumphant man" (p. 129); and he anticipates the
time when science will enable man to "become the master
of all learning, and consequently equal to the great moving
principle" (pp. 223-24). Though certainly superior to Bush in
education and refinement of character, Dr. Bat, whose name
suggests his intellectual blindness, is curiously like him in the
assertion of his own ego and in the assumption that his
mind and will represent the standard for judging the universe. He is similar to the squatter also in that the removal
of civil and religious restraints has encouraged the development of selfish desires, for Dr. Bat is much more interested
in garnering personal fame than in modestly increasing human
knowledge.

This is not to say, of course, that Cooper denies the legitimate aims of freedom and knowledge in his portrayal of
Bush and Bat, for all the evidence of his life and works clearly
indicates his devotion to freedom and his respect for true

science.[17] What he *is* attacking is the arrogance—both physical and intellectual—of undisciplined men. Through the character of the trapper, he reveals the basis for its control. In *The Prairie*, the trapper is more specifically religious than he had been in the previous books—in *The Pioneers* he had turned away from the Reverend Mr. Grant's church—but his moral view of the world remains unchanged. His experience in the untamed wilderness has convinced him of his smallness in relation to God's universe, has developed in him a deep spirit of humility, and has endowed him with a true sense of his own limitations. Like Bush, he wants no unnecessary laws—the fewer the better—for he knows how men can distort the injunctions of God to their own willful ends. But unlike Bush, he desires his freedom not to gratify his own passionate wishes but to exert willingly that principle of self-discipline and self-government which lies at the heart of both true religion and true democracy.

By the end of *The Prairie*, the problem that Leatherstocking has had to face is abundantly clear. Distrustful of the social and civil law on the one hand, he detests the aberrations of freedom as revealed in Ishmael Bush and Obed Bat on the other. He has achieved the self-discipline he needs to lead a free and asocial life, but he has also learned that few others can attain by themselves the same desirable end. He has sought the woods to practice the kind of life he loves, but every step he takes westward opens a path for the exploiters who follow him. At last, driven to the Great Plains "by a species of desperate resignation" (pp. viii-ix), he dies physically defeated; but intellectually and morally he still maintains his deeply felt philosophy. That the attitude toward the universe which the trapper affirms ought to animate the lives of those who follow him is clearly the meaning of the three books. That human nature being what it is, men will not follow his moral path is equally certain. If they do not, however, men face a serious question of whether or not a free society can survive on a selfishly despoiled and wasted continent. In his three early tales of the wilderness, therefore, Cooper penetrated to the heart of the American experience and raised questions that were to disturb him for the greater part of his career.

VII   *Minor Novels*

The Prairie was completed in Paris where Cooper had taken his family in the summer of 1826, and the last three of his tales of the American past—*The Red Rover* (1827), *The Wept of Wish-ton-Wish* (1829), and *The Water-Witch* (1830) —were all written in Europe where the Coopers lived until the fall of 1833.[18] Two of these books are very disappointing; *The Red Rover* and *The Water-Witch* are particularly weak in that Cooper departs from themes with which he had been so successful to compose a pair of tales of the romantic, swashbuckling variety. These two novels, fundamentally alike in plot, technique, and meaning, we may treat together; but we defer until later the discussion of *The Wept of Wish-ton-Wish,* which is entirely different.[19] The two tales of the sea have in common exciting adventure involving a pair of out- laws—a pirate in *The Red Rover,* a smuggler in *The Water- Witch*—and thrilling pursuit by the legal authorities. They also contain unfortunate attempts by Cooper to justify his outlaws through illegitimate appeals to the patriotism of his readers.

Both Captain Heidegger—the Red Rover—and the Skimmer of the Seas—the smuggler—are accomplished gentlemen, gen- erous to their enemies, and honorable and true to their friends. Men of culture and education, they frequently turn out to have much higher principles than respectable men on shore. But although Cooper charms us with his pictures of attractive rogues, he is not content to let the books go as pleasant fantasy. Since he seems to feel that he must give a reasonable explanation of their attractiveness, we are seriously told that the Rover became a pirate because, while serving in the British navy, he had fought and killed his captain who had insulted the Colonies. In 1759, he is already dreaming of a free America, and he redeems himself finally by his death in a naval engagement in the Revolutionary War. If we take this as seriously as Cooper presents it, we are drawn to the conclusion that piracy is justified if the motives are properly patriotic! Apart from this lapse, however, we can still con- sider *The Red Rover,* in Brady's words, as a "gay sea pastoral" in which romantic adventure is its sole excuse for being (p. 75).

The Water-Witch includes a similar justification of its rogue, who, Cooper would have us believe, is a smuggler only because the British laws for colonial commerce are so unjust (p. 408). This appeal, however, is not the main fault in the tale. Much more serious is the complicated apparatus of supernatural trappings that invest the ship: a glowing figurehead, oracular prophecies, and strangely disappearing lights. To the extent that one can suspend his disbelief, he may accept the tale—in Winters' words—as a kind of "comic opera" in which "the style is adjusted to the plot in a manner at once brilliant and meticulous" (p. 47). Most readers will agree with Grossman, however, that although the book has virtues— the magnificent rhetoric of Myndert Van Beverout is a major one—the supernatural elements are grossly overdone; that, in addition, too much is realistically explained by Cooper to allow us to accept as fantasy those parts which are not (p. 71). The light touch was never Cooper's forte; he always succeeded better when he grounded his theme firmly on objective reality.

Such is surely the conclusion we must draw when we read the novels in their order of composition and come upon *The Wept of Wish-ton-Wish* between these light romances. This somber tale of Puritan New England has never been properly understood by its critics. Lounsbury thought the picture of the Puritans unfair (p. 75); Winters praised only the Indian characters (pp. 42-43); and Grossman, while accepting the depiction of the Puritans, centers his discussion solely on the latter half of the book (pp. 68-70). All have failed to penetrate its meaning because they have not perceived the function served by the two most important elements in the tale: the frontier setting and the religious background that Cooper provides. Careful reading of Cooper's early successes, however, should alert the reader to the significance of the densely realistic background; furthermore, the religious undercurrent to be observed in many of those works should prepare him also for serious consideration of a religious theme when it animates the entire action of a tale. The critics are right in observing that Cooper was never sympathetic with the Puritan view; they are wrong when they entirely ignore the significance of the religious theme.

For *The Wept of Wish-ton-Wish* is not so much a Puritan as a broadly Christian book full of biting ironies that make telling comments about true and false religion. And the contrast between the two has much to say as well about the theme of American expansion that Cooper had already treated in the Leatherstocking tales. Laid on the Connecticut frontier in the late seventeenth century, the novel shows a stage of the process even earlier than that of *The Last of the Mohicans*. Mark Heathcote, a stern Puritan who, twenty years before, had left England during the Civil War, has established a frontier settlement just at the limits of civilization and conceals in his blockhouse one of the regicides. Strict, autocratic, superstitious, and convinced of his own election though he may be, Heathcote is an impressive character with so strong a faith as not to be "unmanned by any vicissitude of human fortune" (p. 16). True Christian as well as doctrinaire Puritan, Heathcote practices his religion with deep resignation and humility; and, even more important for the story, he acts his belief among the red men. He has bought his land fairly from the Indian tribe that owned it; and, as his son tells Metacom (King Philip) toward the end of the book, "in this valley hath wrong never been done to the red man" (p. 356).

The valley of the Wish-ton-Wish is, therefore, an isolated world of faith and justice which is beset on one side by the revengeful agents of Charles II who come searching for the regicide, and on the other by the Indians, Wampanoags and Narragansetts, who see themselves being pushed from their lands by the greed of the white men and who make no distinction between the just and the unjust settlers. Conanchet's father, Miantonimoh, had been killed by the Pequods and English; and, though still a boy, Conanchet comes to the settlement seeking revenge. He falls into the hands of the Heathcotes, who, rendering good for ill, take care of the boy and teach him of the Christian God; and Conanchet comes to see that there is "much honesty in them within" (p. 362). Nonetheless, although guiltless of all wrong, the settlers of the Wish-ton-Wish are attacked by the Indians, who, returning ill for good, fight their way into the settlement, capture one daughter and a witless boy, free Conanchet, and drive the Heathcotes into the blockhouse, which they burn around their heads. Cooper deliberately leads the reader to believe, as the Indians do, that the Heathcotes have been burned to death. But they do not die in the fire. Within the blockhouse was a deep well in which the settlers had taken final refuge. In a magnificent chapter developed through carefully handled symbolism, which unaccountably has been missed by the critics, the characters arise one by one from the well as from the womb of earth in an obvious symbol of birth. Phoenix-like, the settlement of the Wish-ton-Wish rises again from its ashes. But the crisis also has its spiritual and moral overtones. If ever people have occasion for bitterness, the Heathcotes certainly do. Yet in a most impressive scene by the open graves of the dead, the tough old Puritan submits to the will of God; lays aside forever all thoughts of vengeance against the Indians; and makes each member of his colony do the same because he believes that "this seeming evil [hath] been ordered that good may come thereof" (p. 236). The colony is physically reborn out of disaster, and the Heathcotes, spiritually reborn as well in their forgiveness of their enemies, begin life anew.

Twelve years pass and the colony prospers. The Heathcotes weep for their lost Ruth;[20] and, although they seek her among the tribes, they receive no word of her. Conanchet, of course, thinks the whole family is dead. More important, however, are the changes that come over the colony, for new voices begin to be heard: Dr. Ergot, a rationalist with a faith in science and progress like that of Dr. Bat in *The Prairie;* and the Reverend Meek Wolfe, an arrogant minister who represents the type of Puritanism that Cooper detests. The humility of the Heathcotes becomes spiritual pride in Meek Wolfe, who deems himself an agent of God and confuses God's will with his own. It is but a step from seeing himself as an instrument of God's vengeance to seeing his own spirit of vengeance as God's! When in a second attack on the valley, Conanchet recognizes the Heathcotes, spares the family, returns their daughter, and renders good for good, Wolfe incites the colonists against the Indians; in essence, he preaches vengeance and returns evil for evil.

And when Conanchet falls into the hands of Wolfe and his kind, they turn him over to Uncas, their Mohican ally, for execution and absolve themselves of responsibility by having the Indian kill him. In so doing, they return evil for good, the direct opposite of the Christian injunction.

Christianity, therefore, Cooper clearly implies, should lead the believer to fair treatment of the Indian and humble submission of self to the harsh realities of life. Difficult as it is for them to do so, the Heathcotes not only forgive their enemies but also swallow their pride and accept the infant son of Conanchet that Ruth has borne in the forest (pp. 420-21);[21] certainly, such true religion ought to lead only to good. But the arrogant new settlers, incited by the Reverend Wolfe, do not act like Christians. They wrong the very Indian who was fairest to the whites; and, in their pride and vengeance, they destroy the tribes and seize their lands—as their descendants were to do for two hundred years across the continent. Conanchet is unjustly killed; his tribe is broken; Ruth dies of the shock of recovering her white identity, and all potentiality for good is lost. By implication, American society has been false to the Christian principles that so many Americans profess. The unjust treatment of the Indians will continue, the initial wrong will be repeated over and over, and the peace that finally settles over the valley of the Wish-ton-Wish will have been bought by evil. Might conquers, justice suffers—and all in the name of God. The Heathcote ideal of dedicating the wilderness to the service of God—a view not really very different from the philosophy of Leather-stocking—has been lost because of the passions of men.

To move from *The Wept of Wish-ton-Wish* to *The Water-Witch* is, therefore, a great disappointment if one wants more from novel reading than the comic opera pleasantries of the latter book. Yet leaving aside Cooper's three unsuccessful or trivial tales about the American past—*Lionel Lincoln, The Red Rover,* and *The Water-Witch*—the decade 1821-1830 marks a period of highly original and intellectually important work. In the six books that remain, Cooper had launched a very successful career, proved that an American could live by his pen, and created half a dozen works of art that can be read with enjoyment and profit over a century later. The

key to his success, it seems to me, lies in his keen eye for the
details of American reality and his uncompromising integrity
that allowed him to probe the implications of that reality
until it yielded interpretations that still have the ring of
truth. To see these ten productive years as evidence of his
patriotism is, therefore, an oversimplification—unless we
mean by patriotism the love of country that can recognize
its gross faults along with its real virtues.

In that sense, Cooper was always patriotic. In *The Spy*
and *The Pilot* he could recognize virtue and honor in the
British camp and see vice among the Americans without
denying the essential rightness of their cause. And he could
view with unconcealed horror the destruction of so much
of the bounty of nature in the westward movement of the
pioneers without denying the validity of that expansion in
the values of Christian civilization that were to replace those
of the wilderness. To Cooper, Americans are not always right
—indeed, they are almost invariably wrong in their treatment of the Indians; but he notes a fundamental truth in
the process of change that should eventually yield a strong,
free, democratic state. From the very first, Cooper affirms
the reasonable patriotism that, no matter what the provoca-
tion, he was never to deny. It is established in these first
American novels; and, even though he was, as in *Home as
Found,* sometimes to be most critical of American ways,
such patriotism remained a dominant theme in his work
until his death.

Other themes as well are foreshadowed in these early
tales. The conflict of appearance and reality which we found
in *The Spy* appears again later in such works as *Wyandotté*
and *Afloat and Ashore.* The divided loyalties one sees in
Lionel Lincoln reappear in *The Two Admirals,* and Leatherstocking is reborn in *The Pathfinder* and *The Deerslayer.*
Criticism of American life and the aberrations of the American
dream also form a staple of much of his later fiction; and the
religious theme, muted in *The Spy* and the Leatherstocking
tales and fully orchestrated in *The Wept of Wish-ton-Wish,*
recurs with increasing importance toward the end of his
career. Cooper established, therefore, in the American novels
of his first decade the characteristic themes and attitudes that

animated his fiction for twenty more years. This is not to say, as some critics seem to imply, that his later books are repetitions of the earlier, or that his first ones are his only truly important ones. Cooper's ideas, like his art, developed as he grew older; and, if *The Prairie* is more sophisticated than *The Pioneers* and if *The Wept of Wish-ton-Wish* is intellectually more complex than *The Spy*, we may expect a continuing development in his later career.

Finally, in the matter of technique, Cooper's early work is original and significant. To be sure, he borrowed many of the tired devices of romantic fiction for his fundamental plots. All critics have observed the recurring patterns of chase and flight, of pursuit and rescue of maidens in distress, and of the return of the lost heir; and these must be considered flaws in his major work. One should not let these conventions, however, blind him to the manner in which Cooper establishes his themes. Fundamental to most of these books is the physical setting involved—a setting described with meticulous care and used as a basic element in the development of the theme. The sea he had not fully learned to use; his best maritime novels, *Afloat and Ashore* and *Miles Wallingford*, were still to come. But the neutral ground in *The Spy* and the natural wilderness in the Leatherstocking tales and *The Wept of Wish-ton-Wish* afforded him the means for a serious examination of important problems and for the presentation of significant themes about the central issues of American life. Granted the time and place in which he wrote, we could hardly ask more of him.

CHAPTER 3

Europe and the United States

B Y THE TIME *The Water-Witch* was completed in the summer of 1830, Cooper had already spent four years of a European sojourn that was finally to extend to seven. For varying periods of time he had lived in England, France, Switzerland, Italy, and Germany and had traveled in the Low Countries and through the Rhineland. Always an acute observer, Cooper had not only seen the usual tourist sights; he had also pondered about the manners and morals of the countries he had visited. This European experience was crucial in Cooper's intellectual and artistic life, for he was quick to perceive that what he observed in Europe had implications for America as well. Indeed, he even came to believe that without a knowledge of Europe, Americans could not fully understand their country's institutions; it was only by comparison that the real advantages of America could be judged.[1] If this belief is true—and most will agree that it is— Cooper was well qualified to speak about American institutions, for he knew Europe intimately. He perceived that the true basis of the British government was aristocratic with power in the hands of the few; he early foresaw that the monarchy of Louis Philippe was designed to place political power in France in the hands of a similar class; and he clearly understood the evils of aristocratic societies as they had existed in Venice and Berne.

I *Prejudiced Conceptions*

Like the patriotic American he always was, Cooper opposed such aristocratic systems and was always ready to defend American principles. He found in Europe an appalling ignorance of America and gross prejudice against American things in general. Wide currency was given to the misconceptions, superficial observations, and condescending conclusions of English travelers who had been to America. "Some forty-odd" such works, as Spiller has shown (p. 127), had already appeared when Cooper wrote his *Notions of the Americans* (1828), a volume written at Lafayette's repeated request and designed as a corrective to the usual European view. The book has been criticized as painting perhaps too happy a picture of the American condition because it actually contains a paean of almost unqualified praise, but it does illustrate quite well that there was more to be said for America than most European travelers were willing to admit. In addition, Cooper helped further the cause of republican principles not only by his work on the American Polish Committee to aid the Poles in their struggle for freedom[2] but also by his part in the French finance controversy of 1831-32 in which he attempted to demonstrate that the expenses of a republic are not greater than those of a monarchy.[3]

But it was not only the Europeans who had misconceptions about America. Many Americans, Cooper felt, had the wrong opinion of Europe—especially of England—and were not at all aware of what true American principles really were. Too many were taken in by the glitter of British society, and far too few were sufficiently independent of European opinion. Although he had pretended that Americans were indifferent to European criticism when he wrote the *Notions,* he well knew that such American intellectual independence of Europe had not yet been achieved. He proposed, therefore, to warn Americans against the evils he clearly saw in European society and to impress upon them the true advantages they enjoyed by virtue of their republican form of government. Since, however, they had to know Europe to understand America, he decided to write a series of European novels to illustrate the dangers of an aristocratic society with money and power in the hands of a self-perpetuating class. Americans, he felt, should perceive these truths so that they might well count their blessings, and, incidentally, avoid the development of such a moneyed and powerful class in their own United States.

This idea quite obviously gave a new direction to Cooper's work. He turned away completely from the physical reality of the American scene that had given such a firm basis to his American novels, and he substituted in its place the description of social organizations with which his audience was not so familiar. Unfortunately, the sense of the background does not always come through; and our reaction as we read the European tales is that, except for *The Bravo*, which develops its theme from a well-drawn objective reality, the works are more important for their intellectual content than for their artistic expression. Moreover, when Cooper returned to the United States in 1833, he was horrified by the direction American democracy had taken and began to instruct his countrymen about proper American principles as well by writing a series of books—*The Monikins, Homeward Bound,* and *Home as Found*—that are even more badly theme-ridden. In none of them did he achieve the degree of objective density that had characterized his earlier work. Indeed, it was not until he returned to the American past in *The Pathfinder* and *The Deerslayer* that he can truly be said to have found a suitable vehicle for the social concepts he developed in Europe and which he wanted to communicate to the American people.

II   *The Bravo*

In *The Bravo* (1831), his first attempt to depict European reality, Cooper was eminently successful. Venice, the scene of the tale, had taken deep hold of his imagination when he was there briefly in 1830;[4] and he found in the organization of the state as it existed at the time of his tale (early eighteenth century) precisely the material he wanted to illustrate the grave dangers of an aristocracy that makes the state the instrument of its own policies. Power is concentrated in the hands of the few. The Doge is merely a figurehead, the real power residing in the Senate and its secret Council of Three. Although it calls itself a republic, Venice is actually a commercial oligarchy; all questions are answered in terms of profit to the state and the hereditary patrician class that runs it. The evil machinations of this group are well represented by the setting of the novel, which Cooper exploits as successfully as he had the native American landscape in his earlier tales. The brilliant exterior of Venice with its picturesque architecture, gay carnivals, and impressive ceremonies such as the marriage of Venice to the Adriatic, conceals a devious, labyrinthine interior, well symbolized by the maze of intricate passages and dark chambers through which the characters move when they enter the public buildings (p. 413).

Just as the state itself wears a mask to hide the reality from prying eyes, so also do the characters frequently go masked in the streets—a custom which alone makes life tolerable in Venice—and the rulers themselves are so well disciplined that their naked faces and avowed words conceal their inner thoughts behind a fair exterior. This disparity between appearance and reality is worked out in all stages of the plot, which is itself as labyrinthine as the devious policy of the state and as full of concealed motives, some of which are finally revealed only at the end of the novel. Thus, the Senate pretends to hear the plea of Don Camillo Monforte for recognition of his claims to inheritance in Venice, but he has been held in waiting for five years while his case is being decided. What stands in his way is the fact that he is a powerful noble outside of Venice, and Venetian law forbids a patrician to own land in other states. Simple justice demands that Don Camillo's plea be granted, but Venice, jealous of preserving its tight oligarchy, refuses to include in its number members who might be too independent of its rule. Nevertheless, his plea is not denied, for the Senate hopes to turn his suit to its advantage.

Don Camillo is in love with Donna Violetta, the ward of a senator. She in turn is a wealthy heiress who cannot be given in marriage to someone in a foreign state without specific permission of the Senate lest he gain influence in Venice. Although both she and Don Camillo are treated with outward respect, it is quite obvious that both are being used as tools of a policy that subordinates all individual wishes to the advantage of an almost deified class. "The sparrow does not fall in Venice," says one of the senators, "without the loss touching the parental feelings of the senate" (p. 86); and this paternalistic attitude which justifies state interference in the personal lives of its citizens is frighteningly like the horrors of modern totalitarianism. Even the senators themselves are not immune. Signor Gradenigo, a member of the Secret Three, is closely questioned by his two partners about the conduct of his son who seeks to wed Donna Violetta for her wealth. No part of the community is free from the prying eyes of the spies that the Senate employs to keep the patrician class in absolute power. To be sure, Don Camillo and Donna Violetta manage to escape the snares that are laid for them and to seek protection in the Papal States; but, for most, escape from such a system is not possible.

Old Antonio, for example, a poor fisherman, pleads with such vehemence for a young grandson impressed in the galleys that he is murdered for openly and persistently questioning the absolute right of the state to do as it pleases. When his friends rise to protest his death, the state cynically gives him a lavish funeral and convinces the poor fishermen that Jacopo Frontoni, a reputed bravo, has killed Antonio. Jacopo had himself fallen into the power of the Senate by proving his imprisoned father innocent of the crime of smuggling. In the hope of having his father freed, Jacopo became a state spy and masquerades to the public as a hired assassin. But the state cannot retract its errors; when Jacopo has outlived his usefulness, he is falsely accused of the murder of Antonio and, in a great show of justice, sentenced to death. Father Anselmo, however, a Carmelite monk, knows the truth since he heard Antonio's confession just before his death and was an unwilling witness to his murder. He appeals to the Doge, along with Gelsomina, Jacopo's fiancée, and they seem assured of success. But just as they think reprieve has come in a signal from the Doge, Jacopo is beheaded in a triumph of Venetian cynicism; the Carmelite is spirited away in the crowd by agents of Don Camillo.

The Bravo is a remarkable book, not only because it is so sound an analysis of the evils of totalitarianism—the modern reader, with Marius Bewley, recognizes it as a predecessor of *1984* (p. 58)—but also for the artistry with which it is developed. Once again, as in his previous novels, Cooper was able to generate an important theme from the realities of his material. But, for the first time, the realities are not the natural scene but a complex social organization. To a great degree

The Bravo is much more sophisticated than the "American" novels; it also reveals how much Cooper learned from his observation in Europe. Although another might have seen in his material only the form of the republic and the external glitter of Venice, Cooper penetrated to the reality that lay beneath—just as he penetrated the monarchy of England and that of Louis Philippe to the aristocratic reality which in the latter case had stolen the July Revolution from the people.[5] Indeed, one might assert, with Bewley, that the novel points to America as well and warns Americans of the dangers that a financial oligarchy would present should it once gain power in America.[6] Be that as it may, the social reality of *The Bravo* is drawn with the same verisimilitude of detail and it has as much dense realism and symbolic import as the American wilderness or the sea; but the theme is more complex than any Cooper had yet developed.

Such a conclusion is clearly shown by a comparison with *The Spy*, a tale which *The Bravo* resembles in its use of the contrast between appearance and reality; in the masks, real or feigned, which the characters wear; and in the analysis of the economic motives that impel Venice and that impelled Mr. Wharton and the Skinners. Even Jacopo, the pariah, bears some resemblance to Harvey Birch; both conceal a virtuous reality beneath the appearance of duplicity and evil. But the meaning of *The Bravo* is much more profound. The theme of unjust justice deliberately courted so that a patrician class, once in power, may perpetuate itself has more significant ramifications for both Europe and America than the ideal of simple patriotism affirmed in the earlier tale. Besides, Cooper has in *The Bravo* the artistic integrity to end his narrative unhappily by allowing Jacopo to be killed unjustly as both the meaning and the artistry of the book demand. Yet it is clear that the line of development from *The Spy* to *The Bravo* is a direct one. If the latter is in many ways the more interesting book, its success derives from Cooper's deep insight into the moral complexities of a sophisticated social organization. In achieving that understanding and in presenting his theme in terms of so well-drawn a reality, Cooper made a real step forward in his development as a serious artist.

III Social Analysis

Many years were to pass before Cooper was again to achieve so fine an artistic success. The two remaining European novels—*The Headsman* and *The Heidenmauer*—are not nearly so well integrated as *The Bravo* but they are extremely interesting for the social analysis they contain. To be sure, Cooper develops his themes once more from the realities of social situations, but in neither did he find a symbol so artistically satisfying as the state of Venice, and in *The Headsman* he managed his conclusion badly to provide a happy ending. Yet both are worth reading today for their shrewd analysis of society and the motivations of men. *The Heidenmauer* (1832) is particularly significant for its depiction of the dangers inherent in an aristocracy—hereditary or commercial—when it throws off the restraint of principle and makes profit and its own security the only ends in life. Although the Catholic-Lutheran struggle is in the background of the novel, the religious question, as Bewley has correctly pointed out,[7] is not central to the book. Cooper studiously refuses to take sides about purely religious issues; indeed, he even goes out of his way to defend many aspects of Catholicism; he makes his most admirable characters consistently devout Catholics: Father Arnolph, the saintly Prior of Limburg; Ulrike Frey, the Burgomaster's wife; and Odo von Ritterstein, the penitent knight.

Rather, Cooper makes a special point of calling the reader's attention to the real theme: the way in which human passions override principle and in which reason becomes rationalization, once moral considerations are ignored and money and power become the sole goals in life. Just as the Venetian senators in *The Bravo* subvert justice for profit and subordinate morality to state policy, so also do many of the characters in *The Heidenmauer* allow principle to be lost when worldly matters are at stake. To illustrate his point, Cooper creates three contending powers in a limited area in Germany, powers that can no longer exist in peace in a changing world. Two of them, the Abbot of Limburg and the Count of Hartenburg have long been in conflict over feudal rights; the third, the Burgomaster of Duerckheim, represents the rising commercial interests that conflict with both. All three represent, therefore, power groups that, once infected by worldly desires, must come into conflict; and, as the times necessarily dictate, the Abbey becomes the prey of Count and Burgomaster, who see in the political and religious confusion in Germany their chance to do away with a powerful rival.

Their task is made all the easier by the worldly Abbot Bonifacius, intelligent and shrewd, but hardly a holy man —as his drinking bout with Emich, Count of Hartenburg, to settle feudal rights well illustrates. He is one of those who, Cooper recognized, used the Church for personal advantage and so brought it under attack (pp. 102-3). Yet the unworthiness of some of the Benedictines does not justify the attack on the monastery. The Count and the Burgomaster are not their judges; indeed, they are men of the same stamp. The gross and worldly Burgomaster, Heinrich Frey, lives only for money (p. 419); and he seeks his justification in half-hearted Lutheranism at the very time he goes on a pilgrimage to the Catholic shrine at Einsiedlen to propitiate the Church and avoid making reparation for the wrong he has done. Essentially he plays both sides so that he may hang on to his gold. Yet Heinrich is foiled in his attempt to be free of a master; for, once the Abbey is destroyed, Emich immediately asserts his authority over the burghers and brings them under his control. He too has followed only his passions in destroying Limburg, because the monks posed a threat to his power. Always seeking political advantage, he even tries to make political capital out of his pilgrimage (pp. 362-63), and he uses the Lutheran revolt to escape the consequences of his act of gross aggression.

Opposed to these devious and worldly characters who have made power and profit their ends in life are the three devout characters. Father Arnolph, who practices the humility and mercy that adherence to his religion demands, serves as a symbol of true principle; Ulrike lives a life of Christian charity; and Odo von Ritterstein, the true penitent as opposed to the false ones, Emich and Frey, has spent a life of penance for an act of sacrilege he had committed at Limburg many years before. The contrast between Odo and the conspirators is deliberately pointed up by Cooper, for the Abbey is sacked by Count and Burgomaster just as a mass is being said in reparation for Odo's sin. Emich and Frey repeat his sacrilege, profit from it, and seek their justification in Lutheranism. Odo, however, turns his back on all worldly things and bequeaths his possessions to a youth who saves his life in the Abbey fire. This youth, it turns out, ultimately marries Frey's daughter, and the Burgomaster thus profits doubly from his act! He and the Count clearly represent the uncontrolled human beings who, freed from the restraint of principle, have no trouble in finding reasons for doing what they want to do. The selfish can always rationalize their selfishness.

Although *The Heidenmauer* is obviously the equal of *The Bravo* in the soundness of the social analysis, artistically it falls far short of its predecessor. Lacking a central symbol so perfectly adapted to the theme as Venice is in *The Bravo*, *The Heidenmauer* is much more diffuse. There are, of course, the obvious symbols of abbey and castle; high on their respective hills, they dominate the town of Duerckheim in the valley below; and the clear intimation is that, when one is destroyed, the other will completely dominate the town. But the effect of this symbolism is dissipated after the sack of the abbey, and the long pilgrimage to Einsiedlen does not quite make up for the dramatic tension that has been lost. The effect is also weakened by the happy ending of the tale in the marriage of the young lovers. Although that union has its irony, the book has been so serious an analysis of human passions and greedy motivations that the wedding bells strike a dissonant note. Cooper employed no device to bring home the theme equal to the beheading of Jacopo in *The Bravo*. Besides, as Grossman has observed, Cooper assumed a quietness of tone in writing this book that is not entirely becoming to him (p. 81); he needed a form that would have done greater justice to his truly important theme.

Similar criticism can be leveled against *The Headsman* (1833), a novel that begins extremely well, but is another which Cooper sadly bungled in its conclusion. Like *The Bravo*, *The Headsman* details the evils that derive from the concentration of power in a self-perpetuating oligarchy. Like Venice, the canton of Berne is ruled by a class of aristocrats with hereditary privilege who naturally want to maintain their position. To Baron Melchior de Willading, it is right and just that he inherit wealth and position; and Peter Hofmeister, the bailiff of Vévey, is loud in his praise of the order of society that has given him privileged status. Indeed, he even goes so far as to assert that the business of government is to protect itself lest such an order be changed—an opinion that the senators of Venice would certainly have supported. Position and privilege, however, Cooper argues, are always bought at a price; and, if some inherit hereditary advantage, others inherit disadvantage. Such is Balthazar, hereditary Headsman of Berne, a mild and peaceful man who hates the distasteful job he must perform. Because of his inescapable office, he is so detested by the populace that he has become a pariah. Jonah-like, he is almost thrown overboard during a storm on Lake Geneva because of the superstitious fear of the seamen and passengers. He has tried to conceal his children lest the curse pass on to them, and he suffers the ignominy of seeing his daughter repudiated at the altar when her lineage becomes known.

Cooper seems, therefore, to be developing the theme that there is little relation between inherited position and ability or virtue. The conclusion is unmistakable that if Balthazar, who learned his bloody trade with the utmost difficulty, is hardly suited for the position that society thrusts on him, many of those in more favorable positions are equally unsuited to the advantages they have inherited. Balthazar's supposed son, Sigismund, a mercenary soldier, is truly fine and noble; and Maso, an Italian smuggler, reveals qualities of truth and honor far above his apparent position. The well-born characters are made to perceive the value of these men when Sigismund saves Adelheid de Willading, the Baron's daughter, and when he and Maso rescue the Baron and his Genoese friend Grimaldi when they are swept overboard during the storm on the lake. Certainly Sigismund is clearly the intellectual and moral superior of the bailiff of Vévey, although the latter holds a privileged position and although the former is at best a mercenary soldier who believes himself to be the son of the Headsman. Adelheid too learns the truth of inherited position; for, falling in love with Sigismund and ig-

norant of his descent, she conspires with her father to arrange
a title for him so that they might marry. But when they
learn that he is the Headsman's son, they experience serious
second thoughts about such an alliance.

As long as the Baron can accept the boy on his merit alone,
he sees nothing to stand in the way of the marriage. They
owe him so much, he argues, "even to our lives" that "we
should be ready to sacrifice every feeling of prejudice, or
habits—all that we possess, aye, even to our pride" (p. 205).
Brave words, and the Baron means them; for, by every true
standard of morality and taste, the match is suitable. But when
the Baron learns that Sigismund must one day assume the
detested position of Headsman, he can only exclaim: "Hath
the villain dared to steal into my family-circle, concealing
this disgusting and disgraceful fact! . . . There is something
exceeding mere duplicity in this, Signor Grimaldi. There is a
dark and meaning crime" (p. 207). Grimaldi, a voice of
reason, however, draws the appropriate conclusion, one that
may well be taken as a statement of the position that Cooper
wishes to affirm: "While every principle would seem to say
that each must stand or fall by his own good or evil deeds,
that men are to be honored as they merit, every device of
human institutions is exerted to achieve the opposite. This is
exalted, because his ancestry is noble; that condemned for no
better reason than that he is born vile. . . . our boasted philosophy and right are no more than unblushing mockeries, at
which the very devils laugh!" (p. 211).

Developed thus far, the theme is a good one; but Cooper
lacked the courage he showed in *The Bravo* and sacrificed his
meaning to a happy ending. In a complicated series of ex-
planations that take place high in the Alps at the Hospice of
St. Bernard, Sigismund is revealed to be only the adopted
son of Balthazar. His true father turns out to be Signor Grimaldi, who, having wronged the girl he married, was punished by the kidnaping of his infant son. In addition, Maso
the smuggler, whom Grimaldi had once believed his true
heir, is really an illegitimate son by a second girl he had
wronged. Sigismund is thus freed from the taint of his foster
father's occupation and becomes once more a suitable match
for Adelheid! Although Adelheid's problem of marriage is

[66]

solved by this manipulation of characters, her protest that she had already decided to marry Sigismund anyway rings false; it never has to stand the hard test of consequences. Such a dénouement is so much romantic claptrap, and one wonders how Cooper could seriously have written it. Indeed, what is worse, it invalidates the excellent theme he has been developing. If Sigismund and Maso are Grimaldi's sons, are we to conclude that their noble qualities are accounted for by descent after all? The serious social issue that Cooper had been developing is irreparably damaged.

It is unfortunate that Cooper could not bring *The Headsman* to a better conclusion, for there are some excellent things in the book. The carefully drawn symbolism of the boat on Lake Geneva which Cooper treats as a microcosm (pp. 70-71, 184) and the mountain at the end that typifies the removal of false social distinctions before the majesty of God revealed in the natural splendor (p. 480) clearly illustrate that Cooper consciously sought appropriate symbolic representation of his ideas. If he did not succeed in giving his concept the same degree of objective reality he achieved in *The Bravo* (the social structure of Berne never comes through so clearly as that of Venice), he found reasonably satisfactory substitutes in these minor symbols. The whole concept of inherited disadvantage embodied in the office of Headsman is an excellent one; and, although Balthazar is somewhat sentimentalized, Cooper makes his plight convincing to the reader. Indeed, so completely real is the dilemma which Baron de Willading and his daughter face that Cooper should have let the book proceed to its logical and inexorable conclusion. In a society of this sort, there can be no convenient escape for his characters. In providing them with one, Cooper marred his book beyond repair.

When Cooper was still at work on *The Bravo*, he had thought that he would probably write some half dozen more European tales, but before he was half way through *The Headsman*, he had already decided that it was to be his final novel.[8] His last two European books had not been well received, and he found himself under attack at home for his part in the finance controversy. Convinced that he had been badly treated by the failure of American officials in France to support him in that affair—one of them actually took the opposing side—and believing that the American press was quoting with approval foreign attacks upon him, Cooper determined to bid farewell to his public in *A Letter to His Countrymen* (1834), which describes his ill treatment by the American press and makes an eloquent plea for American intellectual independence. To Cooper's mind, the value of his three European tales was their analysis of Old World society. By showing the evils inherent in aristocratic systems, he affirmed the value of the democratic principles by which Americans lived. When the books did not succeed, Cooper complained that the American public approved his work only when he wrote of American things, but turned away when he began to write of American principles. Since American critical opinion was so far under the influence of foreign theories as to refuse to receive him with favor, he believed he had no choice but to give up his profession.

IV Criticism of America

Cooper, of course, did not stop writing. An astonishing number of books came from his pen during the next few years, but at first none of them could really be called novels. Moreover, his purpose had sharply changed. Cooper's return to America in 1833 was as crucial an experience in his intellectual career as had been his sojourn in Europe; the United States of 1833 was not the country he had left in 1826. In the leveling and uninstructed democracy that he saw developing, Cooper recognized a grave danger to true republican principles; in the development of political parties, danger to intelligent and disinterested government; in the rising commercial class, loss of the sense of values that had characterized an agrarian society. In the face of such evidence, his purpose became clear. Not only had he to warn his countrymen of the dangers inherent in the European system, he had also to instruct them in the true principles of American democracy, which he believed were being subverted by the new developments in American society. At first, in *The Monikins* and his travel volumes, he attempted to fulfill both of these purposes at once; but, as the decade wore on

and he came to be more and more in conflict with his countrymen, he devoted his attention increasingly to the criticism
of American life.

In *The Monikins*, published in 1835, though actually in
preparation before he left Europe, Cooper develops both of
his themes. Hardly a novel, the book is really a piece of social
satire in which the story is completely subordinated to social
purpose. It has had few defenders. Lounsbury boasted that he
was the only man in his generation to have read it through
(p. 134); and more recent—and more sympathetic—critics have
been in total disagreement concerning its merits. Spiller
dismisses all the introductory matter as too prolix and concentrates on the social satire presented through the Monikin
(monkey-manikin) societies of Leaphigh and Leaplow (pp.
237-38). Grossman, on the other hand, prefers the jaunty introduction to the less spritely monkey world that follows
(p. 96). Justification exists, of course, for both opinions. The
introduction is perhaps too much drawn out, but it does
introduce us to a Cooper who has a real sense of humor;
and, although the satire in the second half may occasionally
be too minute, it does bring his concepts of European and
American society into direct contrast; and, in Spiller's words,
it contains "the freshest and most concise statement of what
its author had learned during his years in Europe" (p. 243).
It is, therefore, an extremely important book in the development of Cooper's thought.

The story is told in the first person by John Goldencalf,
an Englishman whose father had been a London waif of unknown ancestry. His whole life completely absorbed in business, the elder Goldencalf had prospered immensely. Beauti-
fully and consistently drawn through the eyes of his son,
Thomas exists solely for the accumulation of possessions. He
is tempted to break a deathbed promise to his wife because
it is going to cost him money; he comes to believe, like the
Venetian senators, that the state exists only for the protection
of property; his final words are "gold—gold!" (p. 59). His
son, however, is reared by a clergyman and comes to develop a "stake in society" theory that he immediately puts
into practice. If only he who has a financial stake in society
is fit to govern, then he with the biggest stake is clearly

the most eligible to rule. John Goldencalf, therefore, carries the theory to a logical extreme by multiplying his interests across the world from the South Sea islands to a Mississippi plantation until he alone of all men "was fit to govern . . . to advise, to dictate to most of the people of Christiandom." He had taken an interest in their welfares by making them his own (p. 86). To be sure, Cooper's irony is heavy, but it clearly illustrates the danger of basing the foundations of government on the possession of property or wealth.

The rest of the book serves a double purpose. It presents the education of John Goldencalf about men and government until he awakes from his delusion; and it embodies a satiric attack on society in England and the United States, both of which are based on selfish interest. For these purposes, Cooper turns John Goldencalf into a kind of rich but benevolent Gulliver, and he brings him to the land of the Monikins, a race of monkeys who have evolved from men and have established a civilization deep in Antarctica. Cooper develops his satire in a number of directions, but most of it involves the social and political systems in two Monikin countries: Leaphigh (England) and Leaplow (the United States). Leaphigh, ostensibly a monarchy, has actually developed a caste system with power in the hands of an aristocracy. Such a system, which Cooper saw at the heart of British society, produces all the evils and injustice that he had depicted in his three European novels. But the aristocracy of Leaphigh has so improved upon the concept of limited monarchy that the king is no longer even a figurehead. Like Orwell's Big Brother, he doesn't even exist! He is a fiction maintained through the use of an empty throne concealed behind red curtains.

Leaplow, on the other hand, is a republic; and Cooper is careful to show that its fundamental principles are sound. Goldencalf begins to see that a government based on property benefits only the moneyed class; that, if government is designed for the general good of all, all must have a voice in its management. Not, of course, that Leaplow is perfect. Cooper heaps his scorn upon it too, but only because its good qualities have been perverted. It should be guided by principle, but it isn't. Instead it is ruled by parties, and Cooper's description of party politics is devastating even today. It should be independent of false aristocratic notions, but it eagerly apes the opinions of Leaphigh; its pretentious citizens fawn upon foreigners and they also derogate native principles while defending even the meanest of native things. During the great moral eclipse toward the end of the book, the people become so completely motivated by economic interests that "there was no dealing with any subject that could not resolve itself into dollars, by means of the customary exchanges" (p. 404). In short, the government becomes unduly influenced by the commercial interests; and it soon begins to turn itself, as under the circumstances Cooper argues it always must, into the "exclusive, or aristocratic" kind (p. 408).

Both England and America are, therefore, subjected to scathing criticism throughout *The Monikins,* yet the detailed allusions can hardly be considered the main purpose of the book. Underlying both attacks is a firm foundation of principle, which becomes apparent when we realize that in both cases the basis for criticism is the same: the attempt by people with money and power to manipulate government to their own ends. John Goldencalf finally perceives this truth in his final summary of what he has learned during his sojourn among the Monikins: that those entrusted with power will abuse it; that a society must divide the trust to minimize the abuses; "that love of money is an 'earthy' quality, and not to be confided in as the controlling power of a state; and, finally, that the social-stake system is radically wrong, inasmuch as it is no more than carrying out a principle that is in itself defective" (p. 427). He had seen these truths illustrated in his father's misspent life, had perceived them again in Monikin society, and had begun to detect them at last in his own dealings in economics and government. He returns to England a wiser man with few illusions about government and about human beings who in a democracy should operate by principle, but who usually act only from selfish interest.

The Monikins is, therefore, a better-integrated book than any of its critics would have us believe; for, despite all its faults, it manages to make its point in a telling manner. Yet one can well understand why the book was never popular. The criticism was likely to alienate large sections of its reading public from the Anglophile to the super-patriot, and it probably also offended that class of Cooper's country-men who based their claims to distinction upon commercial success. Cooper's attack upon all the failings of America is everywhere devastating; full of biting irony; and, in some spots, quite funny. But if Cooper's attack is essentially true, it is also rather tactless. It simply could not be expected to appeal to an American audience of the 1830's; and, as Gross-man suspects, it may even have prejudiced his readers against the clearer expression of the same ideas in the books that followed it (p. 97). Nonetheless, the book is not so unread-able as critical opinion would suggest. To be sure, the allegory of England and America should perhaps be less minute, and the broader issues involved be placed in a clearer light. Yet if we approach it with the proper detachment, we find not only that large sections are thoroughly enjoyable but that, as Winters has pointed out, parts are extremely well written (pp. 26, 33).

V *Travel Books; Democratic Teachings*

With the failure of *The Monikins*, Cooper turned away from even the semi-fictional presentation of his ideas and prepared for the press a series of travel volumes—*Sketches of Switzerland,* Parts I and II (1836); *Gleanings in Europe: [France]*, and *Gleanings in Europe: England* (both 1837); and *Gleanings in Europe: Italy* (1838)—in which social criticism of both Europe and America is scattered among the descrip-tions of the many sights he had seen. Like *The Monikins,* however, they were unsuccessful; and Cooper sought yet another form for the exposition of his theories. In a well-thought-out and systematically organized political essay, *The American Democrat* (1838), he set out to instruct his country-men in what true democratic principles really are. His return to the United States had convinced him that the most serious danger to American democracy lay in the people themselves. The fundamental issue is one that troubles social thinkers even today: how to control the leveling tendencies of a democracy to insure the protection of the intelligent and educated élite that is obviously needed to provide leadership and direction to society. Cooper bases his theory upon a Jeffersonian belief in the natural inequality of men, and he supports the democratic order as the only one that gives the talented man a chance to rise.

Yet the very organization of a democratic society militates against such a process. If the majority can impose its will upon the society as a whole, the intelligent élite will be drowned in a sea of mediocrity; and power will fall into the hands of demagogues who can manipulate the majority as they will. To offset these dangerous tendencies, Cooper argues that the will of the majority is not absolute. Though it perforce must rule in the political sphere, it must always act under the constitutional restraints designed to insure the safety of the indispensable minority, and it must never be allowed to substitute public opinion for law. Restraint of the majority, in Cooper's view, is as essential in a democracy as is restraint of monarch or aristocrats under any of the European systems. Cooper knew whereof he spoke: he had already come into conflict with his neighbors in Cooperstown over a piece of land—Three Mile Point—that had been used on sufferance by the townspeople while the Coopers were away and which the citizens came to believe belonged to the people themselves. Cooper had seen not only a meeting of the people disregard his complaints but their "majority" opinion supported in the partisan Whig press. It was a small matter, but Cooper saw at stake in the controversy an important principle.

Cooper answered the attacks in a number of ways. He tried at first to reply in the Democratic press; next, to return to a fictional presentation of his views in *Homeward Bound* and *Home as Found;* and, when the latter volume incited his enemies further to personal attack, to take legal action in the courts because of their libels. Cooper's legal struggle against the power of a politically inspired press,[9] a struggle which he largely won, is long and involved and needs no repetition here. It is important, however, in that it led him back to fiction for the development of his ideas and provided a realistic background for his next two tales. Cooper returned to novel writing with *Homeward Bound* and *Home as Found* (1838),[10] a pair of tales that, inspired by the Three Mile

Point controversy, are more important for their intellectual content than for the means of expression. Yet weak as the novels certainly are artistically, both are essential to an understanding of Cooper's development. The events of the years since his last true novels had sharply altered his purpose. He had begun the decade warning Americans against the dangers of Europe. Now he was to try to warn them against themselves.

Originally these two novels had been planned as a single book showing the reactions of an American family when it returns home after an extended stay in Europe. The Effinghams, descended from the Elizabeth Temple and Oliver Effingham of *The Pioneers,* thus have the knowledge of Europe required for a thorough understanding of the United States and can seriously evaluate American virtues and faults. But as Cooper began to write, he was carried away with the adventure part of the tale. Captain Truck of the American packet *Montauk,* justly suspicious of British arrogance and jealous of American sovereignty, refuses to answer the hail of a British man-of-war as he sails from Portsmouth and then makes a run for the open Atlantic. Pursued by the British ship *Foam,* the *Montauk* has to maneuver too far south and in a tempest is dismasted off the coast of Africa. After a thrilling struggle with the Arabs, the ship replaces its masts with some taken from a wreck, sails for New York, and meets the *Foam* off Sandy Hook. There Captain Truck surrenders an English embezzler to the British authorities; the British captain, for an undisclosed reason, takes Paul Powis, a cabin passenger, from the ship; and the novel ends just at the place where Cooper had planned to begin it: with the landing of the Effinghams in New York.

Yet quite apart from the adventure story, *Homeward Bound* is significant in that it brings into direct contrast typical English and American types; furthermore, it adumbrates, as Spiller has observed, the international theme that Henry James was to develop a generation later (p. 259). Mr. Sharp, actually Sir George Templemore traveling under his servant's name, can accept the Effinghams as his social and intellectual equals; for European and American gentlemen are one about manners and morals. But the English are less liberal and more affected by national prejudices than their American counterparts, for to a man they are condescending to America. Even at the other end of the scale, there are differences. Mr. Monday, a lower-class Englishman, compensates for his mediocre life in drink; Steadfast Dodge, an American newspaper editor, seeks his compensation in a frantic struggle for gain and public approval. In this class the English come off somewhat better, for Monday knows his place and has none of the aggressive arrogance of the lower-class American. In the fight against the Arabs, Monday is at least courageous, but Dodge is both a physical and moral coward.

The main purpose of the book, however, is not so much illustration of national differences as criticism of American failings. Most of the satire is directed against the ill-mannered, ignorant, egotistical Steadfast Dodge, who sways with the majority opinion he helps to create and is totally unaware of any of the civilizing graces. A leveling democrat who admits no superiority in a fellow countryman, Dodge fawns over aristocrats, even over the false George Templemore who is actually the embezzler in disguise. Totally incompetent to form a just opinion about anything he has seen, he has kept a journal which he hopes to publish on his return and which reveals his appalling ignorance of Europe. Dodge, however, is the kind of democrat who believes one man's opinion is as good as another's and who loves to operate through the manipulation of committees. To show the folly of the man and his ideas, Cooper sets the honest, straightforward Captain Truck against him. As he had done in *The Pilot*, Cooper uses the captain to show that there is need for absolute authority in areas where majority opinion, uninformed and uninstructed, is valueless. When Dodge tries to meddle in the affairs of the ship, the captain promptly puts him and his committee down. The point, as Grossman has noted, is almost too easily made (p. 117); but it is essential since it clearly establishes one of the limits of democracy: there are areas where authority is needed.

The issue is developed further with the Effingham family— Edward and John, who are cousins, and Edward's daughter, Eve. Their opinions, based upon sound principle and firm knowledge, are clearly worth more than Dodge's in almost any area; and their views of both Europe and America must necessarily be more sound. Of course they differ considerably among themselves: Edward and Eve somewhat stiffly defend their country, and John rather cynically warns of their impending disappointment. Proud, sarcastic, conscious of his own obvious superiority over other men, "Cousin Jack" is not entirely a sympathetic character, and Cooper rather flaunts him before his readers. Yet John Effingham has his virtues. A harsh critic of American society, he nonetheless remains a true republican, and although he is far from humble in his attitude toward other men, he exhibits a sincere humility before his God. Edward, on the other hand, though equally independent of thought, is much more tolerant of American failings. He too can perceive the weakness of America, but he loves his native land so much that he remains its sincere advocate at home and abroad. In many ways, he is Judge Temple of *The Pioneers*, the Christian gentleman, living on into an age that leaves him vulnerable to the attack of the democratic levelers.

Yet despite the sharpness and accuracy of Cooper's comments about American democracy, *Homeward Bound* leaves much to be desired as a work of art. Cooper was not able to unify the social and adventure parts of his book. The use of a ship under sail to bring together a wide range of social types is clearly a happy invention, for the very closeness of the quarters presents some serious problems. But much of the effect is lost in the long and exciting struggle against the elements and the Arabs. Moreover, Cooper engages once again in the romantic cliché of the handsome stranger, Paul Powis, who appears to be something other than what he seems; who has a deep mystery in his background; and who, presumably under a cloud, is taken off the American ship by the captain of the *Foam*. It is also obvious that Paul and Eve are attracted to each other and that Cooper is up to his old trick of complicated plotting that marred so many of his books. Thus, although *Homeward Bound* has had its defenders—Grossman in particular likes the adventure part (p. 119)—the book clearly shows that Cooper had failed once again to find a vehicle worthy of the seriousness of his theme.

Home as Found is hardly more successful. A continuation

of *Homeward Bound,* the book brings the characters to Templeton and solves the mystery of Paul Powis, who eventually turns out to be John Effingham's son by a secret marriage. Paul and Eve are, of course, married; and Sir George Templemore is paired off with Eve's cousin Grace Van Cortlandt. At best, the plot line is thin; at worst, rather melodramatic; and the value of the book lies not in the story but in the analysis of American society and in the vignettes and characters it presents. The Effinghams, loyal Americans despite what they criticize in their country, continue to represent what ought to be the top of American society—republicans in politics, but much superior to the mass in background, education, and experience; and, therefore, the intellectual leaders of society. All three are opposed to hereditary aristocracy, believe that all men should have a chance to rise by merit, and regard democracy as the best means to assure the rise of those who most deserve advancement. John remains the professed cynic, humble only before God; Eve stiffly represents the height of the intellectual but feminine American woman; and the wooden Edward continues generally tolerant of and forbearing with the people's excesses.

Included in the book as well are many more American types who run the whole gamut of society in both town and country. In New York, we find both the social-climbing Mrs. Jarvis as well as the well-bred Mrs. Hawker. We see in Grace Van Cortlandt the best an American girl who has never been to Europe can become, and in Miss Ring, who frantically tries to hold the attention of beaux who would really prefer to talk about business, the vulgar pretension to polite society. The anxious Miss Ring, desperately seeking popularity, the climbing Mrs. Jarvis, and the "literary" Mrs. Legend are still recognizable American types; and the men, the plain-living and unpretentious Jarvis as well as those completely absorbed in trade, are fundamentally as true a picture of one segment of American society as they were in the 1830's. In the country, too, we find some recognizable characters in the downright vulgar gossip, Mrs. Abbott, who will lend her name as willingly as she will a cup of sugar. She is the female counterpart of Steadfast Dodge; for both are pious-seeming, patriotic-sounding, vicious scandalmongers who are seared by envy of all above them and who try to pull everyone down to their own level. We meet the Anglophile, Mr. Howel, who will believe anything that emanates from England, and the super-patriot, Mr. Wenham, who considers America at the very pinnacle in all things. We even have the local character, the Commodore, a kind of domesticated Leatherstocking.

The best-drawn and most important of all the characters however, is Aristabulus Bragg, a man, Cooper comments, who is "an epitome of all that is good and all that is bad, in a very large class of his fellow citizens" (p. 19). Though undeniably a talented man, the land-agent of Templeton has all the vulgar prejudices of his class. A firm believer in equality and progress, he values all things by their price; and he admits distinction only in the matters of wealth and political preferment. A born manipulator of men, he can persuade a group of apprentices that it is more democratic to play ball in the street than to trespass on the Effingham lawns, yet he defers abjectly to popular opinion and can scarcely believe that a majority could be wrong. Bragg, who aspires to the top, has qualities that could take him far; but he has enjoyed none of the advantages that in another society would have made him "a gentleman, a scholar, and one who could have contributed largely to the welfare and tastes of his fellow-creatures. That such was not his fate was more his misfortune than his fault, for his plastic character had readily taken the impression of those things that from pro-pinquity alone pressed hardest on it" (p. 254). Bragg is the unfortunate but unknowing victim of the democratic state. He has risen somewhat in society because of his talents. The pity is that he had neither the model nor the means for rising higher. He typifies the American high average of achievement bought at the sacrifice of any real excellence, a point that Cooper repeatedly makes in the novel.

In both *Homeward Bound* and *Home as Found,* of course, Cooper does more than view with alarm the failures and excesses of democratic society; for, along with his attacks, he attempts to indicate what the cure should be. First of all, he insists that American principles must be understood. Majority rule applies only to government; it does not apply at all in any other sphere; and Cooper goes out· of his way to establish this point. A majority opinion means nothing if the decision is not in accord with the truth. A committee may decide that a piece of land, like the Three Mile Point, belongs to the people; but what is the value of that opinion in the face of a legal deed to the contrary? Democracy is a means to an end, Cooper consistently argues. The end sought is liberty for the individual, not the unrestrained sway of popular opinion. Increasingly in his work, Cooper saw this belief as implying that some principle of restraint must be applied to fallible men, and that democracy must somehow be seen in religious terms so that men may be impressed by their own need for a deep humility before something that is clearly beyond them. Only in this way, he seems to say, can society keep ignorant mediocrity from being so self-assertive as it becomes in men like Steadfast Dodge.

Cooper saw little hope of such humility developing out of the left-wing Protestant churches dominant in the America of his era. If any man may interpret the truth as he will and if ministers preach by "stirring people up" emotionally, Americans faced the danger of subverting Christian principles to satisfy their personal desires. Therefore, throughout *Home as Found*, he criticizes those churches that put the convenience of the people before worship of God and which refuse to bend the knee even to the Deity.[11] His superior characters, like the Effinghams, always belong to a strictly organized, conservative church in which the people have no right to change belief as they please. Although aware of their own superiority over other human beings, they humble themselves before God; and, conscious of their own fallibility, they try to dominate no one. Thus, while Cooper clearly asserts the value of a political democracy, he places limits on its social manifestations and he argues for the leadership of the educated, informed, intelligent, yet humble Christian gentleman. Cooper's point was not understood by many in his generation, and the Whig newspapers were merciless in their attacks on him. More serious than this reaction, however, from the literary point of view, was Cooper's own failure to find a better means for expressing his ideas than the series of incidents in simple time sequence that forms the structure of this intellectually sound but artistically weak novel.

VI Return to the American Past

Cooper himself recognized his failure in these novels. In the preface to *Home as Found*, he had written that the depiction of contemporary American manners was an almost hopeless task since the nation was characterized "by a respectable mediocrity"; but he was making the attempt "with a perfect consciousness of all its difficulties, and with scarcely a hope of success" (p. vi). That he stated the true cause of the novel's failure may perhaps be questioned, yet Cooper did turn away from the contemporary scene in his next three tales to develop his themes through the kind of material with which he had won his early success—the American past.[12] Of the three, the middle one, *Mercedes of Castile* (1840), a slow-paced story of the discovery of America, must be quickly passed over as the worst mature novel that he wrote. Despite the inherent drama of Columbus' first voyage, the book is intolerably dull; the lifeless characters recite long set speeches to one another; and Columbus, like Washington in *The Spy*, is dignified to the point of woodenness and helps set the tone of pompous solemnity from which the book never really emerges. Cooper was not at his best when writing true historical romance. He was always much more successful when dealing with a kind of symbolic history— a fact easily substantiated by turning from the dull *Mercedes* to the last two Leatherstocking tales, which precede and follow it in the Cooper canon: *The Pathfinder* (1840) and *The Deerslayer* (1841).

These two tales, concerning as they do the career of Leatherstocking thirteen years after Cooper had laid him to rest on the prairie, present the critic with a double problem. Obviously they are related to the three tales that had already been written in the series. But they must always be seen too in the immediate context of Cooper's work. Thus, if *The Pathfinder* is conditioned by what Cooper had written in the earlier tales, it is also strongly influenced by *Home as Found*. It is certainly a different book than it would have been had Cooper written it when he first conceived the idea in 1831[13] before his return from Europe. The relation to the three early Leatherstocking tales is clear enough, not only in the reappearance of the characters of Natty Bumppo (here called Pathfinder) and Chingachgook but also in Cooper's return to the natural landscape to dominate the tone of his book. Repeatedly stressing the sublimity of both forest and lake, he clearly makes the point that the power of God revealed in each should teach the lesson of humility to all who see themselves in relation to the natural wilderness. The themes of the American waste of nature, of the unjust displacement of the red men, of the march of civilization across the continent, and of the insecurity of the white man in the virgin wilderness are present in *The Pathfinder* as they were in *The Last of the Mohicans* and *The Prairie.*

These themes, however, are muted in *The Pathfinder.* The fundamental purpose of the book is something far closer to the central issue in the "Home" volumes than to anything in the early wilderness tales. The real problem of the book is social but in the "manners" connotation of that word. This primary interest is somewhat obscured by the familiar wilderness material and by the relatively low social position of the characters: they are much below the level of the Effinghams. Nevertheless, their problem is similar. Cooper insists that social station is important at *all* levels of society since class lines exist everywhere; and, although they are not rigidly fixed, they are not to be crossed with impunity. Class, of course, is never purely hereditary with Cooper; for, although one tends to belong to the class of his father, people can rise above or fall below the station into which they were born. Cooper stresses the fact that each person has his appropriate gifts and special knowledge, and that to overstep the limits thus placed on everyone will usually lead to disaster. Cap, for example, is a salt-water sailor who cannot command successfully on Lake Ontario, for his knowledge and experience are not equal to the task. When he tries to command the *Scud* in place of Jasper Western, a Great Lakes sailor, he almost runs the ship aground. It is saved only when Jasper assumes command. In the practical world, each must act in accordance with his talents, knowledge, and experience.

In the less tangible world of social relations, the same truth is equally manifest. Lieutenant Muir, the uxorious quartermaster, has fallen below his proper station because of his numerous marriages and his less formal liaisons with women; Mabel Dunham, the sergeant's daughter, has been educated beyond the point that would make her a suitable match for a common soldier, but she has not attained sufficient knowledge and sophistication to be an officer's lady (pp. 115-16). Her problem, therefore, is a difficult one; for in a military garrison there are few eligible suitors for her hand. Hence, the central theme of the book is a peculiarly social one—proper marriage for the heroine; but the problem is set against a highly unusual background. In the wilderness outpost, of course, Mabel becomes the center of attention of a wide variety of men. Arrowhead, a Tuscarora chief, is attracted to her; Lieutenant Muir becomes her suitor; and Pathfinder and Jasper Western become rivals for her hand. The former two are obviously unsuitable; and the sergeant, totally unaware of the position his daughter has achieved (pp. 307-8), and judging suitability solely by his own masculine standards, encourages the suit of Pathfinder. The simple woodsman, for the first time called Adam-like at the very moment that Cooper tries to humanize him (p. 143), so far forgets himself as to let the sergeant persuade him to hope for Mabel's love.

Cooper's use of Leatherstocking in such a social context has been much commented upon by the critics; and Zoellner, in particular, has pointed out that *The Pathfinder* really does not fit in the over-all pattern of the Leatherstocking series (p. 413). Everything that Cooper had written of his character certainly indicated that his forest life, his deep friendship with his male companions, and his function as the symbolic embodiment of the American consciousness forbade his settling down in a cabin with wife and children. Yet Cooper manages to make his attraction to Mabel believable, mainly because, despite his desire, he seems himself somehow reluctant to win her; and his grotesque reaction—half laughter, half weeping—when he is refused convincingly presents the conflict between the two elements in his character, the social and the asocial. On purely material grounds, the match is unsuitable, for it is beyond belief that Pathfinder could adopt the ways of the settlements for very long. Although the sergeant almost exacts from the couple a death-bed promise that they will marry, Pathfinder learns that Mabel and Jasper are in love, gives up his suit, and sees them happily settled in a cabin on the lake. He perceives the truth about himself: he is born to celibacy in the wilderness and could never hope to reach the level of civilization that Mabel and Jasper represent. His "gifts" forbid that he could ever be content with it.

Seen thus in the context of the order of Cooper's novels, *The Pathfinder* has less to say about American expansionism than about American social democracy. Cooper insists upon class lines, but he also maintains that they have nothing to do with political democracy or the inherent value of men. Jasper Western is better educated and more refined than Pathfinder and, as such, is a better match for Mabel. But he is not necessarily a better man. Jasper and Pathfinder are equal in virtue, though different in talent and experience; both are morally superior to Lieutenant Muir, who has had many material advantages in life. Men are different, are unequal, Cooper argues; and each should organize his life with a clear understanding of both his talents and his deficiencies. Jasper is superior on fresh water, Cap on salt, Pathfinder in the woods. If each but stoops to what he knows and can do, with humble submission to the God revealed in the sublimity of forest and sea, all will be well. If men fall into the natural classes determined by the function they can fulfill in life, a just society will result. Indeed, some will rise, just as Jasper and Mabel eventually move into the merchant class in New York (p. 515). It will not be a leveling democracy, however, or one where Steadfast Dodge can operate; it will be truly democratic so long as each is free to find his proper station because of merit alone.

Cooper's choice of the familiar wilderness materials to present his social concepts was a particularly happy one. It removed the issue from the contemporary scene where the sensibilities of his audience were likely to be bruised, yet it really did not change the point he was trying to make. It is likely, of course, that many of his audience missed the theme completely, that they failed to see the relation between this book and *Home as Found*, the one immediately preceding it.[14] The same, quite possibly, might also be said of *The Deerslayer* (1841); for it too is concerned less with the march of American civilization than with the question of popular American values. The last of the Leatherstocking tales to be written, though the first in the chronology of the hero's life, *The Deerslayer* is perhaps the best of the series in the complexity of its meaning and in its affirmation of value in American life. Like *The Pathfinder*, it concentrates on lowly characters and is concerned with considerable social import; but it places much more stress upon moral meaning. The book has a strongly religious tone which provides the series with its final note of affirmation.

The setting of the tale is similar to that of *The Prairie* in its almost perfect wilderness state, but the natural landscape is not nearly so harsh and forbidding. In contrast to the absolute desolation of the earlier book, the Glimmerglass (Otsego Lake) shines like a jewel in the wilderness of trees that stretches west from the Hudson River halfway across the continent. The dominant mood is peace and serenity; and Cooper pauses frequently to stress the quiet of forest and lake at night, at dawn, at high noon—indeed whenever its peace is not shattered by the crack of a rifle or the shrieks of passionate men. It is a landscape "altogether soothing, and of a character to lull the passions into a species of holy calm" (p. 83). It ought to fill all who perceive it with the feeling of reverence and awe for its Creator that, Cooper writes in the preface, had been the dominant influence on the character of Deerslayer; but unfortunately it does not. "I have only studied the hand of God, as it is seen in the hills and the valleys, the mountain-tops, the streams, the forest, and the springs," the woodsman once tells Hetty Hutter (p. 267); but he has learned more from such tuition than have most of the other white characters. Like most Americans, they accept as a matter of course whatever is familiar to them and seldom give it a second thought.

The only man-made objects to be seen on the lake are the ark, a large boat, and the castle of Tom Hutter, a house built on piles out on the water. Cooper makes the castle a kind of microcosm of the moral states possible to men in such a setting. At the bottom of the scale are Tom Hutter and Hurry Harry (Harry March), the former an ex-pirate, the latter a woodsman. Hurry in particular illustrates a number of the most unattractive American traits. He takes great pride in his good looks and physical strength, justifies to himself whatever he wants to do, and throws tantrums when thwarted. He is endlessly restless, as his nickname implies, and he considers members of other races as so many animals. He thus represents an unpleasant side of the American character that is still with us.

Moreover, Hurry and Hutter are as economically motivated as any of Cooper's European villains. Since the only value they respect is money, they will do anything to get it—even to killing women and children to collect the bounty placed on Indian scalps. They are literally in business for all they can get out of it; and in the first attack on the Huron camp they almost scalp Hist, Chingachgook's fiancée, who is a prisoner of the Hurons. Judith, too, Tom's older daughter, is a creature who worships the physical, both in her own beauty and in the glitter of the British officers who sometimes visit the lake. Thus, in a setting that should convince all men of the vanity of their selfish motives, all three characters are determined upon their own willful ends.

Opposed to this view is the affirmation of the Delawares, Deerslayer, and Hetty, Tom's younger daughter. The Indians, of course, live in close communion with nature and follow their own red "gifts" to lead a satisfactory life, but one necessarily far below the Christian ideal that Cooper holds up for his readers. Still, the Indians are morally superior to Tom and Hurry. They scalp for glory; but, since they know no better, they cannot really be blamed. Deerslayer and Hetty, however, affirm a higher good. Both are curiously alike in being unreasoning creatures—Deerslayer is simply an uneducated and generally unthinking man; Hetty, simpleminded from birth. Both are frequently described as childlike, and one cannot escape the impression that they have both achieved the happy state (they have become as little children) that the Gospel of St. Luke describes as the passport to Heaven. Both are removed from the sophisticated temptations of civilized life, and both are somewhat deficient (Deer-slayer is physically unattractive; Hetty, simple-minded) in qualities most frequently praised among men. Despite these handicaps—or perhaps because of them—both try to live their lives in accordance with Christian morality and ethics. As Brady has noted, there is a Dostoevskian quality in these marred but moral beings.[15]

That the completely Christian life which Hetty in particular affirms is all but impossible in a fallen world would seem to be part of the meaning of the book, but the converse is equally true. The totally unchristian life is complete chaos. To illustrate his point, Cooper sends Hetty into the Huron camp to plead for the lives of her father and Hurry, both captured in their scalping expedition against the Indians. Hetty accepts the injunctions of Christ to forgive one's enemies and to turn the other cheek as literal guides to life, and she preaches them to the Indians. She is utterly con-founded, however, when Rivenoak, the Huron chief, asks her why the whites do not follow them themselves—a question that a Christian apologist intellectually stronger than Hetty might have trouble in answering. But if Hetty's course is impractical, her words clearly illustrate how far below the Christian ideal her father has fallen, and how richly he de-serves the fate that the Indians, rendering simple justice, finally mete out to him: they scalp him alive and leave him to suffer and die.

Between these extremes stands Deerslayer, whose practical experience keeps him from trying to live by the ideal ethics that Hetty preaches but whose Christian training at the hands of the Moravians prevents him from engaging in the ghastly occupation of Tom and Hurry. Rather, he follows, as he tells the Indians, the law of nature (rather than the law of God) "to do, lest you should be done by" (p. 538). Deer-slayer is on his first warpath; and, as his name implies, he has heretofore been a hunter, not a warrior. Now, in a beauti-fully written passage that Winters justly praises as among Cooper's best work (pp. 36-37), Deerslayer confronts his first enemy, graciously offers him a chance for his life, and by the quickness of his eye (the dying Indian names him Hawkeye) shoots his first human being. In killing him and a second

Indian, however, Deerslayer is not the aggressor. To be sure, his actions are something less than the Christ-like turning of the other cheek that Hetty tries to preach to the Hurons. But his actions are certainly practical—and they have the universal justification of self-defense.

In this practical world, of course, Hetty cannot survive; for, although she bears a charmed life among the Indians, she is totally incompetent to live in normal society; and the man she loves, Hurry Harry, hardly realizes that she exists, so attracted is he to the beautiful Judith. It is appropriate, therefore, that she be killed accidentally in the final fight, just as it is essentially right that the lovely but tarnished Judith be rejected by Deerslayer when she offers him her love. But if Hetty's standards are impractical, it is equally true that civilized society cannot survive with the standards of Tom and Hurry. The worship of the physical to the detriment of the spiritual (the love of things as opposed to the love of principle which Cooper saw everywhere in American life) and the economic motivation that will condone all acts which bring a profit are both wrong attitudes that can only lead to disaster. Tom and Hurry are the New World counterparts of the Abbot Bonifacius, Count Emich, and Heinrich Frey; and *The Deerslayer* is as eloquent a warning against the subversion of principle for profit as was *The Heidenmauer* or *The Monikins,* or for that matter, the two novels of contemporary manners that he had completed just three years before.

A practical compromise between the best and the worst in men is certainly Deerslayer, who is imperfect and fallible but also, in Brady's words, "an embodied conscience for America" (p. 95). He is a man who sees the moral values of the American landscape and who has absorbed enough from the Moravian missionaries to give that perception a definitely Christian tone. He represents a kind of competent humility, unselfish and unconcerned with the impedimenta of American things; and he affirms American principle by calmly and quietly going his way almost instinctively doing what is right. Uneducated and unreasoning, he clearly shows that virtue does not depend on qualities of mind but may well be corrupted by them. Physically unattractive, he illustrates that a beautiful reality may exist behind an unprepossessing exterior appearance. He lacks, of course, the civilizing qualities of Judge Temple in *The Pioneers*, and one cannot escape the conclusion that the ideal American would somehow combine characteristics of the two. Nevertheless, in this final volume of the Leatherstocking tales, Cooper has developed a character who criticizes in all he says and does the evil realities present in American life.

And yet *The Deerslayer* does not end on a truly optimistic note. To be sure, the Glimmerglass returns to its naturally beautiful state, the selfish characters retire to the fort, and Deerslayer and his Indian friends melt into the wilderness. But the reader of the tale knows what is going to happen: the ideas that Deerslayer affirms here and reaffirms in *The Pathfinder* and *The Last of the Mohicans* will be ignored by his fellow Americans. The struggle between white man and red will be re-enacted for over a century. The settlers will come with axe and gun to chop the trees and slaughter the game in *The Pioneers*, and the earth at last will belong to its despoilers. Ishmael Bush is implicit in the characters of Hurry Harry and Tom Hutter, for they are a constant factor in the American scene and become increasingly important as the wilderness is opened. It is with a kind of nostalgia for what might have been that we see Deerslayer, Chingachgook, and Uncas pass into the wilderness at the end of *The Deerslayer*; for this has been the first stage of the struggle, not only between the whites and Indians, but between the values of Deerslayer and those of Harry March. And we know the result of that conflict: the Harry Marches win.[16]

If we read in these terms, *The Deerslayer* is a much more significant book than Mark Twain's criticism would have us believe. Indeed, it may well be considered Cooper's masterpiece, for it unites in one well-executed whole the dual streams that had been developing in his work: the sense of the American past in both its temporal and spatial aspects and the question of values as they were developing in contemporary American life. *The Deerslayer* is the logical culmination of the Leatherstocking series. It affirms a set of values that were always implicit in the earlier tales; and, with *The Pathfinder*, it applies them by implication to the contemporary American scene. The fully developed religious view everywhere apparent in the book is thoroughly consistent with that expressed in the best of his previous novels. In addition, the economic motivation criticized in the characters of Hurry Harry and Tom Hutter is the same that Cooper had attacked in *The Bravo, The Heidenmauer,* and *The Monikins.* To be sure, Cooper had thrown the scene of the story a century in the past and thus escaped the kind of criticism leveled against the inferior novels that had attempted to describe contemporary manners. But his theme remained the same.

With *The Pathfinder* and *The Deerslayer,* Cooper's work had come full circle. He returned to the material with which he had won his first great success; but the intervening years, difficult and unsuccessful as they certainly had been, were by no means wasted. Cooper's residence in Europe had given a new direction to his thought and provided him with a point of reference from which to judge the changes he saw taking place in American life. The inability of his countrymen to understand or accept his conclusions forced him to organize them in a coherent pattern and to experiment with means for their expression. Surely we can in part thank the difficulties that Cooper experienced in the mid-1830's for that fine little volume of political theory, *The American Democrat.* And his persistence in seeking a form for the presentation of his ideas, though it led him to compose several bad novels like *Homeward Bound* and *Home as Found,* also induced him to experiment once again with his wilderness settings. The result was the last two Leatherstocking tales, the one a thoroughly competent social novel, the other a true masterpiece.

The Pathfinder and *The Deerslayer* thus represent Cooper's recovery of the fine creative gifts that had been largely dissipated in the frustrating years since *The Bravo.* Once again he had managed to draw his physical backgrounds with a convincing degree of verisimilitude; and, more important, he was able to generate a significant theme from the realities among which his characters move. That the themes he develops in the second decade of his authorship are in many ways more fundamental than those he had previously treated bespeaks most clearly his intellectual and artistic development, for the best work of this second decade is superior to that of the first. A more sophisticated Cooper wrote *The Bravo* than *The Spy*; a more skillful artist composed *The Deerslayer* than created *The Pioneers*. Cooper had truly found himself during this long and difficult period. To be sure, he would sometimes err and write weak novels in the years ahead. But the moral theme he had developed in *The Deerslayer* gave an added dimension to his work—one that was to become increasingly important in the tales that immediately followed.

CHAPTER 4

Values in Conflict

W ITH THE last two Leatherstocking tales, Cooper re-
covered completely from the artistic disaster of the
1830's; in effect, he launched a new career in fiction some
twenty years after his first success. But there is not any great
discontinuity in his work: the tales that were to come from
his pen during the next ten years are in both form and theme
a logical development of those he had been writing since
he began *The Spy*. Cooper's late novels are certainly as well
grounded in objective reality as his early ones; and the
themes he treats—the conflict of appearance and reality,
divided loyalties, and the importance of a religious view of
life—were present in his earliest fiction. But if Cooper re-
worked his earlier material in a new series of novels, he
did not repeat himself. Just as *The Deerslayer* is not a repetition of the first Leatherstocking tales but a development
of them, so also are the other novels of the 1840's logical
developments of his earlier work. The divided loyalties of
Lionel Lincoln reappear in *The Two Admirals,* the ambiguous
relations in *The Spy* occur once again in *Wyandotté*. But in
every case, the emphasis has changed; the resolution of the
conflict is not so easily achieved; and the theme embodies a
much more complex moral concept than any in Cooper's first
tales.

I *The Darker View*

Part of the reason for this change, of course, is the age
of the author. The world looks different through the eyes
of fifty than it did through those of thirty, a truth which
Cooper develops in the Miles Wallingford novels; further-

more, Cooper's experience had not been such as to leave him with many of the illusions of youth. Although he remained as patriotic an American as he had been when he created Harvey Birch, he realized too that patriotism is a relatively minor virtue in the scale of moral values: "our country, right or wrong," as he wrote in *Miles Wallingford*, is a mark of spurious patriotism in that it subordinates God to country (p. 204). He remained a democrat, but his experience during the 1830's had clearly illustrated to him the dangers of an unrestricted democracy; and, although he continued to affirm the moral view of nature he had early expressed in the character of Leatherstocking, he saw it increasingly now in more specifically Christian terms. Above all, he came more and more to distrust the ability of fallible men to guide their destinies through the use of reason alone—a view which can be traced from its initial expression in the character of Leatherstocking to its full development in tales like *The Sea Lions*. In effect, Cooper's view of the world became darker as he grew older; he came to see the issues of life as far more complex than they had appeared to be in his earliest fiction.[1]

Thus, Admiral Bluewater in *The Two Admirals* faces a problem of acting patriotically during a bitter conflict; but unlike Harvey Birch, he must sacrifice another loyalty to fulfill his purpose. He faces a dilemma, therefore, which the earlier character had not to reckon with. Similarly, Captain Willoughby of *Wyandotté* encounters a problem as baffling as that faced by Lionel Lincoln; but he cannot solve it by simply sailing to England and leaving it behind. Various conflicting commitments press these later characters on every side so that each action entails a sacrifice that is not easy for a man to make. The mature reader, therefore, although he realizes that Cooper no longer includes so much of the rapidly paced adventure that characterized some of his earlier tales, recognizes in these later works a more faithful representation of the world and of men. None of the late sea novels, perhaps, can touch the romantic excitement that Cooper instilled in *The Red Rover* or *The Pilot*, but tales like *The Two Admirals* or *The Wing-and-Wing* present characters who face more real and pressing human problems. Issues that had once remained in the background come increasingly to the fore, and the problem of acting in accordance with principle becomes more and more difficult to solve.

These later novels, however, are seldom read. Although several seem to have been popular when they first appeared, Cooper failed completely to regain the reputation he had enjoyed when he sailed for Europe in 1826;[2] and, as the 1840's wore on, his alienation from his countrymen came to be almost complete. Many of these novels never enjoyed much critical esteem; for most of Cooper's biographers and critics preferred to stress the historically important early fiction and the socially significant "Home" novels rather than any of the later tales, the Littlepage series alone excepted.[3] Such an emphasis has been unfortunate, for many of these late novels are artistically significant. In some of them, Cooper develops his themes as well as he ever did; for he creates an environment and a set of characters, which, through their interactions, reveal a significant meaning to the problem of life. Several of them are very well integrated, all elements contributing to the development of the theme; and some contain characters who, although they have little of the romantic glamor of Harvey Birch or Natty Bumppo, are real people struggling with the problems of a world which, in its ambivalence and complexity, is strikingly modern.

Such is certainly the world that Cooper depicts in his next five major novels. All of them, recalling the moral ambiguity of the neutral ground in *The Spy*, present a world in which little is what it seems to be; the mask of appearance conceals the nature of the reality that lies beneath. In such an ambiguous world, each man stands in multiple relations to those around him and finds himself at times torn by conflicting values, each of which has a legitimate claim upon his allegiance. Admiral Bluewater, in *The Two Admirals*, must choose between loyalty to the Stuart Pretender in the uprising of '45 and loyalty to his old friend and commanding officer, Sir Gervaise Oakes. Ghita Caraccioli, in *The Wing-and-Wing*, faces a conflict between her Roman Catholicism and her love for the atheist revolutionary, Raoul Yvard. Captain Willoughby, in *Wyandotté*, is brought to an impasse during the Revolution when his family is divided between king and colonies. Each novel presents the problem in a different way and depicts the inevitable consequences of the possible courses of action. Finally, in *Afloat and Ashore* and in *Miles Wallingford,* Cooper develops the theme in full complexity and offers the solution toward which all of his work had been tending: the affirmation of a system of value which must take precedence over all others—no matter how legitimate. These five novels, therefore, are extremely important to an understanding of Cooper's final intellectual position and the development of his art.

II *The Two Admirals*

In the uprising of 1745, the historical background of *The Two Admirals* (1842), Cooper found material that was admirably suited to his purpose. The issue that the Young Pretender raised was one of the rights of legitimacy; for, by all the logic of kingship, he should have been the British sovereign. His appearance in Scotland, therefore, opened a question of loyalty: whom should the patriotic Briton support? To one of the characters in the novel, Richard Bluewater, a rear admiral of a British fleet, the issue is a vital one. He has long secretly considered the Stuarts the rightful heirs to the throne, and he wants the Pretender to succeed. Bluewater's problem, however, is complicated by his rank and position. He commands the rear division of a Channel fleet under the leadership of Sir Gervaise Oakes, a vice-admiral loyal to the Hanoverians, who has received intelligence of naval movements among the French in support of the Pretender's invasion. As a naval officer, Bluewater obeys his superior, follows him into the Channel to intercept the French, but is presented with a difficult moral choice. Either he must be disloyal to his command and to his old friend by withholding his division and letting Oakes be defeated, or he must disobey the dictates of conscience, help Oakes defeat the French, and thus fight indirectly against the Pretender, his proper sovereign.

Bluewater is the only one to face such a dilemma. For most of the other characters, the issue is of little importance. Stowel, the captain of Bluewater's flagship, has served under both Anne and the Georges and sees "but little difference in the duty, the pay, or the rations" (p. 345). Oakes, too, shares this practical attitude, for he will accept whatever *de facto* government he finds above him to maintain the order of society. That Oakes is fundamentally inconsistent in his view, however, is well shown in the subplot of the novel. While the admirals are ashore in Devon, their host, old Sir Wycherly Wychecombe, dies without apparent heir, and the estate is in dispute between the man who has possession, Tom, the bastard son of the baronet's younger brother, Baron Wychecombe, and the legitimate heir, young Wycherly, a Virginian grandson of a still younger brother long thought lost at sea. Young Wycherly is, therefore, in much the same position as the Pretender: he too has come from over the sea to claim his own. Oakes, quick to agree that the legitimate heir be placed in possession of the estate, does all he can to help; but he fails utterly to see the parallel with the Pretender, whose claim is equally just (p. 234).

Bluewater and Sir Reginald Wychecombe, a Jacobite cousin of the family, do see the similarity. If the order of society demands that the rightful heir succeed to the estate, it also demands the accession of the Stuarts to the British throne. To Bluewater, the reasoning is incontrovertible; and he puts to sea half-determined to support the Pretender. But like all men, Bluewater has already somewhat compromised his position. By keeping his thoughts to himself, he has encouraged others to trust in his loyalty to the reigning monarch; and, although he intends to refuse a knighthood offered by George II on the eve of battle, he has accepted promotion in the navy and received command of his ships from the same king. The laws of the navy, moreover, which he has sworn to support, demand obedience to his superior, Sir Gervaise Oakes. Bluewater's problem eventually leads him to an intellectual and emotional impasse that is only resolved by the action of the practical Oakes, who, with Bluewater in the offing with half the ships, engages a French fleet that outnumbers him two to one. Oakes gambles on the belief that Bluewater will not let his old friend be crushed by the French. He is right. At the crucial moment, Bluewater brings up his division, defeats the French, and falls mortally wounded in the battle.

The Two Admirals is a stirring tale of the sea; indeed, it is one of the best of Cooper's maritime novels in its thrilling descriptions of the maneuvers of whole fleets in action. Its main virtue, however, is not the romantic adventure which it certainly contains, but the manner in which the realistic details of plot, character, and setting support a truly significant theme.[4] The problem is a real one that all men face: confronted by conflicting legitimate values, as all men are in this troubled world, how shall men act? The practical man of action, like Oakes, has no trouble. He sets a goal for himself and subordinates everything to that end. Oakes wants to defeat the French and is even willing to presume upon Bluewater's friendship to get him to do what he knows is opposed to his conscience. His reward is success and glory. The more thoughtful Bluewater, however, cannot follow this path. He knows he has defied his conscience for friendship. He has betrayed his lawful sovereign and fought against his sincere belief, acting solely on the human basis of loyalty to an old friend, who, in a sense, has used him for his own purposes. It is an understandable choice, but it is an open question whether it is a right one.

Cooper does not say. He does not commit himself on the morality of Bluewater's action, and some critics have taken his noncommitment as evidence that he was for once supporting the status quo to the detriment of principle: that, in Grossman's words, he persuades us "to the acceptance of the world itself and of things as they are" (p. 160). Such would certainly be a strange position for Cooper to take after fighting so vigorously against the distasteful realities of American life, and it is not really the theme of the book. For although Cooper does not editorialize, the ending itself creates doubt that Bluewater's course was best. To be sure, he dies with honor and is buried in Westminster Abbey, and he retains the gratitude and affection of his old friend, who visits his tomb each year on the anniversary of his death. But in a moving final scene some thirty years after the battle, we see the result of Bluewater's sacrifice. The right of the Stuarts is lost forever; and Oakes, now senile, has forgotten his friend so completely that he must be prompted to recall anything of the past. All the glories of fame and human honor—even the memorial chapel in the Abbey—seem trivial in the face of frail human memory and the endless stretch of eternity. If Oakes himself supplies "an instance of the insufficiency of worldly success to complete the destiny of man" (p. 576), the validity of the sacrifice of principle that Bluewater made to help him achieve that success may well be questioned. His own tomb is certainly an empty honor.

Cooper, of course, neither praises nor blames. He illustrates the problem in a thoroughly convincing action and lets the characters resolve the conflict in human terms. But he makes abundantly clear that Bluewater's solution is bought at the price of a betrayal of principle, just as his following the dictates of conscience would have led him to dishonor among men. Bluewater is placed in an intolerable position; and, like many thoughtful men, he vacillates rather than acts. A man of undeniable good will, he is incapable of making a choice until Oakes forces his hand. But although Bluewater is false to his true belief, his moral failure ironically makes him the more warm and understandable as a human being. There is no moral posturing in the book, no absurd heroism, no easy solutions. The world of *The Two Admirals* affirms none of the simple patriotism of Harvey Birch; it affords no easy solution like *Lionel Lincoln*. Cooper's characters now grapple with a world in which nothing human is entirely right or entirely wrong. The very difficulty of Bluewater's dilemma, therefore, makes his compromise of principle thoroughly understandable. Caught in a similar impasse, who can say he would do otherwise?

III *The Wing-and-Wing*

An equally difficult problem confronts the main characters in Cooper's next novel, *The Wing-and-Wing* (1842). Ghita Caraccioli, an Italian Catholic, and Raoul Yvard, a French revolutionary and an atheist, have met by chance and have fallen in love. The wide difference in faith forms an impassable gulf between them; both are torn between their deeply felt philosophic beliefs and their need to fulfill their love. Neither will concede anything to the other, however, and they soon reach an impasse. Raoul, thoroughly a rationalist, will admit only that some immutable principle is at work in the universe, for his mind can perceive that similar principles do function on earth. He refuses to admit a personal God as either Creator or Savior; and, like Dr. Bat in *The Prairie*, he relies completely on the human mind in all things. In vain does Ghita, who has the deep faith of the devout Catholic, remonstrate with him. To rely on reason alone is, to her, mere human presumption; and Raoul's seeking a God he can understand (p. 165) is only the working of a fatal pride in human reason. There can be no compromise between the beliefs of two such people.[5] To be sure, Raoul is willing to marry her, even before a priest; but she refuses to accept him, clearly recognizing their fundamental incompatibility and fearing that her love for him will lead her to slight the duty that she owes first to God.

All action in the book hinges upon this conflict, for it mirrors the basic drama that is being enacted in the Mediterranean between the aggressively revolutionary France of 1798-99 and the conservative society of Europe represented by the Italian people and the British fleet. Against this background, the struggle of the ill-starred lovers takes place. Raoul carries his suit to Ghita, even running his lugger, the *Wing-and-Wing* (the *Feu Follet*, or Jack O'Lantern, as it is really called), into the enemy harbors to see her. When she goes to Naples to plead for the life of her grandfather, Admiral Caraccioli, who is about to be hanged for treason, Raoul follows her, although Nelson's whole fleet is there. He is captured and sentenced to death as a spy, escapes, runs aground on the Siren's Rocks, and is eventually attacked by the British and killed. To his moment of death, Ghita gently tries to lead him back to faith, but he only goes so far as to concede that chance could not have created the universe (p. 478). Cooper permits him no sudden conversion.

Yet the theme is neither so simple nor so melodramatic as a brief outline of the action would suggest, for Cooper does not oversimplify. Although Raoul is a corsair and an atheist, he is by no means painted as an unprincipled villain. Completely sincere in his belief and thoroughly honorable in all he does, he puts the English themselves to shame when they try to get him to betray his crew for a price. The British officers would scorn him if he took their bribe, but they are not too good to offer it. Indeed, the Christian English even take advantage of the virtue and innocence of Ghita when they trap her under oath and force her to betray her lover. The British fleet, although ostensibly on the side of the angels, actually represents sheer power. Professed believers, the British are sometimes more scrupulous about the legality than about the morality of their actions when their own interests are at stake; and they even refuse to redress an obvious wrong, like the unjust impressment of neutral seamen, if their primary goal might be affected by the action. Instead, they equivocate.

A prime example is their treatment of Ithuel Bolt, a New Englander pressed into British service. No one could ever mistake him for anything but a Yankee; his speech betrays his origin. Indeed, the British seamen themselves on board the frigate confess the truth, for they promptly name him "The Yankee." So shorthanded are the ships, however, and so jealous the rivalry between them that no captain will give up a man once pressed. They maintain the fiction that he is English, therefore, despite the gross injustice they do him. When he escapes to Raoul's ship and is later recaptured, he is threatened with court martial for desertion. But they never try him; they prefer to give some credence to his story and to claim that they want to give him the chance to prove his nationality. All the time, of course, they keep him hard at work under discipline, and no one ever explains how he is to prove his nationality several thousand miles from home. The British, however, have it both ways at once: they have the able seaman they need, and they pretend to show him justice. It is small wonder, therefore, that Bolt hates all English as a nation of hypocrites.

Yet Ithuel Bolt himself equivocates in his moral life. Grossly ignorant of everything that does not come from his own provincial home, he firmly believes all the ignorant slanders about the Catholic Church (pp. 163-65) and proclaims the great superiority of his own form of worship. But although he pretends to belief in his own religion, he is extremely lax in the practice of it. He will lie under oath, something the unbelieving Yvard would scorn to do; and, though he is clearly "law honest," he will smuggle if he thinks he can get away with it. Mean, selfish, revengeful, and cruel, Ithuel Bolt is a rogue, albeit a gravely wronged one, but he does not come to a rogue's end. Rather, he returns to America after many years, in possession of several thousand dollars that he has somehow acquired. Respectable now, he experiences religion, and soon becomes "an active abolitionist, a patron of the temperance cause, teetotally, and a general terror to evil-doers, under the appellation of Deacon Bolt" (p. 486).[6] So do the evil prosper, Cooper seems to say, while the honest perish.

Like *The Two Admirals, The Wing-and-Wing* paints, therefore, a realistic picture of a morally complex world. To the person of principle—and Raoul is clearly one as well as Ghita—the choices presented are never easy. Conflicting principles are forever at war; honest men are torn by values, which, though perhaps good in themselves, are hopelessly contradictory. And as in the previous novel, Cooper admits of no easy solution. Raoul and Ghita can never marry if they remain true to themselves; hence, he dies at the hands of the British, she retires to a convent. Meanwhile, power succeeds, as it always does, whether it is scrupulous or not. The compromising, practical British always prevail; and the scheming Bolt, ever willing to sacrifice belief for gain, eventually wins position, wealth, and power. It is a dark view of the world that Cooper draws in *The Wing-and-Wing;* but it does far more justice to the moral complexity of reality than did so many of the earlier novels which it resembles, most particularly *The Spy, The Water-Witch,* and *The Red Rover.*

Raoul's fate of capture and trial as a spy while trying to serve his beloved Ghita reminds one of the fate of Captain Wharton in *The Spy,* who was also captured while on a personal visit behind enemy lines. But Raoul's problem is never so simple as Wharton's. The love of Ghita complicates his life as the captain's never was; and, in place of the understanding Washington, who actually helps young Wharton to escape, Raoul must face the hard-headed, practical British officers, who would perhaps rather not hang him but who are certainly determined to destroy him. There is less romance in the later book, but far more reality.

In a similar fashion, both ship (*Feu Follet*) and master (Raoul) recall *The Water-Witch* and the Skimmer of the Seas, but without the magic absurdities. And Raoul, the attractive enemy, is certainly blood brother to Captain Heidegger, the Red Rover. But Cooper now avoids the specious morality he saw fit to include in the earlier tale; he is content to let his hero be what he must. Raoul is, therefore, more understandably human and better motivated than the Rover. Above all, he has a true moral problem to solve, and his end, more consistent with the logic of his life, is much more realistic. Cooper comes closer to grips with truer problems of life in the later book, and he writes a far more satisfying novel.

IV *Wyandotté*

An even darker view of reality pervades *Wyandotté* (1843), Cooper's next major work.[7] Like the ones he had published the previous year, this novel also develops the theme of conflicting values, but with a far greater degree of concentration. Cooper returns to the kind of material for which he is best remembered, the American wilderness, and he sets the scene on a land patent in upstate New York at the time of the Revolution. Like the valley of the Wish-ton-Wish, the Willoughby patent is a microcosm, and we are to understand that the problems of this little colony are those of the world at large. The tenants themselves recognize this truth, for they regard their community as a self-sufficient island with little contact with the outside world. The patent includes a fair cross-section of the American population, including Negroes, Indians, Dutch, and Yankees as well as British New Yorkers and Englishmen. Most of the Christian sects—including the Catholics—are represented, as are most of the attitudes toward society likely to be found among men. And the people themselves, both landlord and tenants, are motivated by a variety of conflicting principles.

The Willoughby son, a major in the British army; the mother; and the adopted daughter, Maud—all loyal to King George—are horrified when the news of open rebellion reaches the patent. But the real daughter, Beulah, who is married to

Colonel Beekman of the Continental army, naturally enough supports the American side. Willoughby himself, the owner of the patent, is a retired British captain and a native Briton. Nevertheless, he leans toward the American cause; perceives that there is right on both sides of the question; and, isolated in the wilderness, tries to remain at least neutral in the struggle. Captain Willoughby's reluctance to take sides is the motivating force in the novel which explores the question of inaction in a morally complex situation. The well-intentioned man, we would suppose, might well choose to support neither side of a quarrel when he believes that neither is wholly right. But such objectivity gets the captain into most serious difficulties, and Cooper seems to say that one must act—simply because action is necessary—even though he may have to support a cause in which he does not wholly believe. Willoughby's problem is thus a most serious one— one that every thoughtful man must eventually face.

Captain Willoughby's dilemma is made even more difficult by his own good nature and by his inability to penetrate surface appearance to the true motives of other people. Appearance and reality conflict once again in the people of the patent, and the captain fails to pierce their masks until it is too late. Joel Strides, for example, the overseer, is one who has benefited from ten years of service on the patent. He seems loyal and should be a man whom the captain can trust. But desirous of rising materially in the world, Joel sees his chance in the Revolution. Although he knows Captain Willoughby leans toward the American cause, he deliberately creates subtle doubts in the minds of the other settlers in the hope that, if he can force Willoughby into the British camp, he can profit from the confiscations that will follow. Joel allies himself, therefore, with some American irregulars disguised as Indians and with some real Mohawks, all of whom lay siege to the patent to try to force Willoughby to resist. If he defends his house and family, as he surely must, his resistance can be interpreted as Royalist sympathy and his property seized. During the siege, Joel and most of the settlers desert the Hutted Knoll, the Willoughby house, leaving the family to the mercy of the Indians, who soon get out of hand and carry the house by storm.

Captain Willoughby also has difficulty interpreting the motives of Wyandotté, or Saucy Nick as he is sometimes called, the Tuscarora Indian from whom the book takes its title. Wyandotté, an untribed chief, served with the captain for many years; was instrumental in leading him to the land he now possesses; and remains a sort of informal, drunken retainer of the family. The captain, however, has sometimes in the past put the Indian under military discipline and had him flogged, an injury to his pride and dignity that the Indian cannot forget. Wyandotté is thus torn between a desire to revenge the floggings and a feeling of gratitude toward the wife and daughters who once saved his life during a smallpox epidemic. Willoughby never really understands the Indian's feelings, and his intellectual blindness leads him to disaster. At the moment of crisis, when Wyandotté is helping the captain free his son, who has been imprisoned by the irregulars, Willoughby feels an impulse of distrust. In an attempt to secure the Indian's loyalty, the captain threatens to flog him should he prove false. Wyandotté, enraged at the insult heaped upon previous injuries, kills him on the spot. But in the ensuing fight, the Indian fiercely defends the captain's wife and daughters from death and mutilation; in effect, he satisfies the second of the conflicting emotions that have disturbed him for so many years.

The captain thus falls prey to two serious and related errors. Essentially a fair-minded man, his honesty leads him into trouble. As the leader of a divided house, he refuses to take sides when the times demand commitment; and he is inevitably destroyed in a conflict in which only partisans can survive. A man of good will who cannot penetrate the less admirable motives of others, he places his faith where it is little deserved. His trust of appearance in men like Joel gives him a false sense of security, which is well symbolized by the unhung gates of the Hutted Knoll. For ten years secure gates have been ready for hanging at the one entrance to the fortress-home. A more distrustful and suspicious man than Willoughby would have hung them at once; but years of peace have persuaded him that such caution is unnecessary, and Joel is always at hand to argue that the effort could better be spent in the fields. Joel and the unhung gates come almost to be equated toward the end of the novel, for both represent chinks in the captain's armor. Through the gate at Joel's urging, the tenants melt away; and through the gate, by Joel's overt act, the Mohawks finally storm the Hutted Knoll.

Yet if Captain Willoughby's essential innocence renders him incompetent to cope with an evil, ambiguous world, his son, Bob, is a master at controlling his fate. More ambitious than his father ever was, he chooses his side immediately at the start of the conflict and manages to preserve both his life and his property. Only he and Maud survive the struggle at the Hutted Knoll; both are saved, ironically, by the arrival of Colonel Beekman and by the loyalty of Wyandotté. Bob quickly perceives his awkward position. He has come in disguise on official duty to the home of his father, and he is liable to be arrested as a spy. To escape the imputation, therefore, he quickly marries Maud, with whom he has long been in love, and pretends—in a reversal of Raoul Yvard's situation—that love alone brought him into his compromising position. Moreover, with the patent in danger of confiscation if Bob should now inherit it, he and Maud deed their share to Beulah's and Beekman's infant son, Evert, since his father's rank in the American army will insure its safety. Neither Beekman nor his son survives the war; and, when Bob and his wife return to America some nineteen years later to inspect the property that is theirs again, the British general and baronet is feted by the very class of people who had once attacked his loyal American father in the name of liberty and independence! Bob's duplicity succeeds where his father's honesty had failed.

Read thus far, *Wyandotté* paints as black a picture of the world as Cooper was ever to draw, one in which the fair-minded are destroyed; the guilty, like Joel and his cohorts, escape unpunished; and fundamentally good characters like Bob survive only by duplicity. Yet Cooper does not let the novel end in despair. Through the character of Wyandotté, he affirms a set of more permanent values. The Indian has lived his life in accordance with a barbaric code of revenge; and, although he is finally converted to Christianity, he still retains much of his former belief. Thus, when Bob and Maud return to America and the son first learns the truth of his father's death, Wyandotté confronts him unexpectedly at the captain's grave with a shocking proposal. Indian-fashion, he offers his tomahawk to Bob to take his revenge. Bob, however, like a true Christian, swallows his bitterness and refuses the offer with the words, "May God in heaven forgive the deed, as I now forgive you." Overwhelmed by this spirit of Christian charity, Wyandotté can only answer with the ambiguous "God forgive" and die (p. 521). Christian humility and forgiveness thus mark the close of the book, yet they represent a system of value directly opposed to those followed by most of the characters to achieve their ends.

Wyandotté is, therefore, a far cry from Cooper's earlier tales with similar settings; its merciless realism sets it apart from them. Here are no noble Indians like Uncas or Chingachgook. Wyandotté, a drunken vagabond, speaks a disjointed syntax far different from their sometimes grand rhetoric;[8] and his laconic description of the Battle of Bunker Hill, where he looted the dead, bears little resemblance to the magnificent panorama described in *Lionel Lincoln*. There are none so pure of motive here, none so self-sacrificing as Harvey Birch, no philosopher of the woods like Leatherstocking. Nor is simple American patriotism one of the main values affirmed. It too is darkened by less worthy motives in the characters, and Joel Strides is even more despicable than the Skinners of *The Spy* because he betrays those who trust and rely on him.[9] All men's motives are clouded; fair-mindedness can lead to destruction; duplicity earns its material reward; and honest objectivity and neutrality cannot survive. Nothing on earth, Cooper seems to say, is to be trusted. The only permanent values remain the principles of the Christian faith, but they bring no promise of material success.

V *Miles Wallingford's Lesson*

Not since *The Wept of Wish-ton-Wish* had Cooper written so unpitying a tragedy, nor was he ever again to write so somber a tale. More typical of Cooper's art is the relatively brighter view expressed in his next two books,[10] *Afloat and Ashore* and *Miles Wallingford*, two parts of a single novel.

But Cooper had not changed his mind about the nature of reality; the world is as full of unforeseen dangers as it was in *Wyandotté;* and intelligent choices are no easier for the characters to make than they were in *The Two Admirals* or *The Wing-and-Wing.* The appearance of things is as difficult to penetrate as it ever was, and the motives of men are fully as devious. Yet these are clearly happier books, for they make a stronger affirmation of value than do the previous tales. In the preceding three novels, Cooper had of course ended by seeing the problem he was developing in terms of the religious view that became dominant in his work with *The Deerslayer.* The validity of Bluewater's sacrifice is questioned at the end of *The Two Admirals;* Raoul in *The Wing-and-Wing* is brought closer to spiritual truth just before his death; and *Wyandotté* ends with a powerful, if somewhat extraneous, assertion of Christian values. But in all three books, the positive statement appears as almost an afterthought. In *Afloat and Ashore* and *Miles Wallingford,* on the other hand, the affirmation arises more naturally from the material Cooper develops.

The first half of the story, *Afloat and Ashore* (1844), is concerned primarily with establishing the nature of reality. Told in the first person by Miles Wallingford, a man in his sixties who is looking back over his past, the novel reminds one very much of such tales as Conrad's "Youth." Miles is a man who has seen much of the world and who, like Marlow (and Cooper himself), has lost most of the illusions of youth. Rather conservative in his view, he does not more than half approve of all the changes that have taken place in America since 1800, when he was a young man at sea; and, although he is not foolishly reactionary (he realizes, for example, that steamboats are more efficient than sail, though he detests the hurry they encourage), he longs somewhat fondly for old manners and old customs (pp. 533-34). In the first-person point of view of these novels, Cooper hit upon an excellent device for presenting his theme; for, in the person of the old man looking back on his youth, he not only can conveniently tell the narrative part of the tale but also can interpret the meaning of the action without seeming intrusive.[11] He is able, moreover, to contrast the fervor of twenty with the knowledge and disillusion of sixty and to reveal in one stroke the unending conflict between appearance and reality.

The world that Miles describes is almost as merciless as that in *Wyandotté*. Chance events may make or break a man completely without warning, and the same phenomenon that harms one may help another. Dangerous currents destroy the *John*, the first vessel Miles sails in, and the second, the *Crisis*, is swept through the Straits of Magellan, a difficult passage in any weather, by similar currents, while the captain himself thinks he is still off Cape Horn. Simple mistakes, even though made in good faith, can sometimes be fatal. Miles' father is killed when he mistakenly trusts his weight on a mill-wheel brake he invented and is swept under when it fails to work. Captain Robbins loses the *John* by relying too much on his own theories of navigation; and Captain Williams is killed on board the *Crisis* when, trusting too much to a false sense of security, he fails to penetrate the motives of an Indian, nicknamed Smudge, whom he allows on board in a bay off the northwest Pacific coast of America. Unforeseeable evil is everywhere, and one must be constantly on guard against it. Vessel preys on vessel with only letters of marque to justify the aggression; pirates threaten, and wind and waves are constant dangers. Besides, nature is capricious. Captain Robbins survives both shipwreck and many days at sea in an open boat, only to be swept to his death in sight of Cape May!

In such a world, little is what it seems to be. One man cannot really penetrate the motives and feelings of another, and few are to be trusted. The Indian Smudge puts on a fine show of stupidity when he is allowed on board the *Crisis*, but he actually leads an Indian band that succeeds in getting possession of the ship. Miles' boyhood comrade, Rupert Hardinge, a lad who first persuades him to run away to sea, seems a good friend to Miles and a truehearted suitor for the hand of his sister Grace. But eventually he reveals himself as a selfish, ungrateful coxcomb who deserts his friend, betrays Grace's love, and causes her death. Even with those who mean well, communication is frequently impossible. Miles loves Lucy Hardinge, Rupert's sister, and she returns his affection. But each misunderstands the feelings of the other, and a coldness settles between them. Much of the estrangement is Miles' fault because of his pride and jealousy, but he is not alone in his misunderstanding. Even the Reverend Mr. Hardinge, Miles' guardian and Lucy's father, the innocent Episcopal minister who believes he can perceive so much, fails utterly to see Miles' attachment to his daughter and never realizes his own son's unworthiness. A man of innocent good will, he is like Captain Willoughby in his failure to understand reality.

The action of the book, therefore, describes Miles' education in the ways of the world, both afloat and ashore. The shipboard half, with its obvious reversals of fortune, chance, and sudden death, complements the episodes on land, where similar chance events, though possibly less obvious, are no less certain to occur. The gradual change that takes place in the position of the Hardinges and Wallingfords is an excellent example. The Hardinge family, poor but well-connected, has long depended on the Wallingfords; but, in a typical reversal of fortune, the Wallingfords eventually find themselves far below their old friends who inherit wealth and begin to move in circles well beyond the Wallingfords' reach. In a similar fashion, the British Major Merton and his daughter Emily are fond of Miles when he rescues them from a French prize in the Pacific; but, when the middle-class English family finds itself lionized in New York and doors open to them that are forever closed to Miles, Emily, at least, turns her back on him and marries the apparently wealthy Rupert. Both afloat and ashore, therefore, Miles learns to perceive reality. Danger and reversals of fortune lurk everywhere, what seems and what is are frequently direct opposites, and misunderstandings and misinterpretations forever occur among men.

Cooper, however, does not paint the world as totally black. One island of peace and security remains in Clawbonny, Miles' family estate on the Hudson, which he leaves periodically for the sea to seek fame and fortune. It represents the security of a past (he is the fifth Miles Wallingford to live there), a tradition, a sense of belonging that exists in neither the workaday world nor the false society of New York. And

Clawbonny remains significantly under the guardianship of the good Mr. Hardinge, who represents a similar system of value in his profession. Miles, of course, does not recognize all this as a youth, but the older man who tells the story clearly perceives it in the manner in which he points out the falsity of so many things that men put faith in. Pride in knowledge and strength fail both Robbins and Williams; faith in friendship, as with Miles and Rupert, can often fail; change and misunderstanding can come between even a pair of lovers (Miles and Lucy); and the pursuit of wealth, which infects Miles as well as Rupert, can lead to disaster.

In *Afloat and Ashore,* Cooper, of course, presents no solution to the problem of life in such a world; he reserves until the second volume his resolution of the conflicts that beset Miles. Rather, in this first volume, he draws as convincing a picture of a moral chaos as he did in *Wyandotté* and illustrates the problem of conflicting values more subtly than he did in *The Two Admirals* or *The Wing-and-Wing. Afloat and Ashore,* moreover, goes beyond the other three in that it develops its conflicts in terms of more immediate situations. Here is no impossible dilemma like that faced by Admiral Bluewater, no extremes of values like those in *The Wing-and-Wing,* no unremitted gloom as in *Wyandotté.* The world is the familiar one in which young men make their way and woo their future wives. Both characters and situations are convincingly portrayed, and Cooper for once draws a flesh and blood pair of lovers whose problem is thoroughly realistic and central to the meaning of the book. In the adventurous and ambitious Miles, torn between the security of Clawbonny and the risks of the ocean, and the feminine, practical, unsentimentalized Lucy, by far the most realistic heroine in the novels, Cooper created a pair of characters who are interesting in themselves and whose problems can sustain the weight of thematic meaning with which Cooper invests them.

Miles Wallingford (1844), the second half of the tale, continues to examine the problem of life in a chaotic and illusory world. Lucy and Miles still misunderstand each other's feelings, even though they are much thrown together at Clawbonny when Grace is dying. Indeed, so far has com-

munication between them broken down that when Miles
sails as owner and captain of the *Dawn,* he writes her a
letter which is a masterpiece of ambiguity. Miles half intends
to let Lucy know of his love although he believes she loves
another; but he unconsciously words the letter in such a
way that it can as easily be taken as a statement of love for
Emily Merton (pp. 177-78). A new element of deceptive
appearance, moreover, is introduced in the character of John
Wallingford, Miles' rich cousin from western New York. John
is his only close relative, now Grace is dead, and seems to
be an honest and open fellow. So interested is he, however,
in the final fate of Clawbonny, that Miles half distrusts him.
Nevertheless, he makes John his heir (his bachelor cousin
agreeing to make Miles his own as well); and, anxious to
put to sea again to make his fortune, Miles, giving a mortgage
on Clawbonny as security, borrows a large sum from John
so that he may take a speculative cargo to Europe. Miles
thus places his secure home in jeopardy on the chance of
making money he really does not need.

The voyage Miles takes in the *Dawn* is the crisis of his life.
With him go Neb, the devoted Negro slave who has shared
all his adventures, and Marble, the faithful first mate he has
known since his initial voyage. If Miles succeeds, he will
become an immensely wealthy merchant and will fall per-
manently into the money-making orbit; if he fails, he is
completely ruined. In the world that Cooper has consistently
painted in the novel, chance and the actions of others will
have as much control over his fate as he will himself; but
Miles does not yet fully realize this truth. The lesson is
brought home as he enters the English Channel on his way
to Hamburg in 1803. England and France are at war; and,
since part of his cargo—sugar—has come from French islands,
the British naval officer, into whose hands his ship falls,
seizes him as a prize of war (he will, of course, also profit
handsomely from the forced sale of the cargo!). Miles escapes with his ship in a thrilling episode, only to fall into
the power of a French corsair, who argues his right to seize
the ship because it has once been in British hands. In a
greedy, warring world, where everyone seems out for personal gain, Miles, like Captain Willoughby, learns that neu-

trality is a completely untenable position. Both sides are eager to ruin him for their own greedy ends.

Miles again escapes only to run into a terrible storm in the Irish Sea as he tries to beat his way once again toward Hamburg. By now, Miles should be convinced of the vanity of placing his faith or hopes in material things in a dog-eat-dog world, but Cooper makes his lesson complete. Little by little everything is taken from him. His faithful slave, Neb, is swept from the deck in the launch at the height of the storm; and Marble, the loyal mate, is dragged overboard in the wreck of the masts. Since most of the crew had been taken by the English frigate and the storm has swept off the rest, Miles, his ship sinking from under him, eventually finds himself alone on a raft far out in the Atlantic. All his hopes are blasted in the wreck of the ship; Clawbonny is lost; and Miles is in a perilous position. Adversity brings him to his knees. "I knelt . . ." he writes, "and prayed to that dread Being, with whom, it now appeared to me, I stood alone, in the centre of the universe" (p. 333). All of his powers of seamanship, all of his mind and strength proved unavailing against the power of the Deity as revealed in the storm. Miles humbles himself, submits to the will of God, and sees all that has occurred as not so much the workings of chance as the operation of God's Providence.

Thereafter, Miles' fortunes take a turn for the better. Neb, Marble, and he soon come together, escape once more from the power of the British, and eventually make their way home. Miles, now a pauper and deeply in debt, is thrown into jail, for John Wallingford is dead. In the absence of the promised will, a distant cousin has inherited Clawbonny and is determined to strip Miles of what little he still possesses. Miles soon learns who his true friends are in a false world: Neb and Marble, who stick by him through everything, and Lucy, who comes immediately to his aid. His pride is now humbled at Lucy's true devotion, which recognizes no distinctions of class or wealth between them; and he receives, for once, a happy surprise when the seemingly false John Wallingford proves true. For he did leave a will in town making Miles his heir; and, when it turns up, Miles finds himself not only in possession of Clawbonny once again but also of all of John's wealth as well. Presumably, Miles' experience has made him the kind of person who may best possess such wealth. He knows so well how quickly it can disappear in an uncertain world that he will never place his hopes in it to the detriment of the more permanent faith he acquired alone with his God in the open ocean.

Thus, the affirmation of value that Cooper makes at the end of these volumes is completely consistent with that in the three that preceded them. In an evil world, full of avarice and dissembling, where little is what it seems to be and values sometimes hopelessly conflict, only the divine standard expressed in the Christian religion is to be wholly valued. The things of the world can disappear in a moment; and, if they do not, they form but a hollow mockery of true value. Men frequently prove false, especially if they stand to gain by their treachery; and, if some do prove true, we have no way of knowing that they will until we have run the risk of their defection in a moment of crisis. All that a man can do in such a world is place his faith in God and seek his happiness with those few people who, like Lucy, Mr. Hardinge, Neb, and Marble, have proved their devotion by their acts. Nothing else can be trusted, not even one's self in mind or body. One's own motives are not always entirely clear to himself, nor can he always perform what he thinks he can. Miles perceives this truth through a life of parallel experience afloat and ashore, and although he ends a somewhat disillusioned old man, he has learned the hard way what the lasting values of life really are.

VI *A Major Theme*

In these five late novels, therefore, Cooper gives full expression to a line of thought, which, although it had been developing for many years in his works, had become a major theme only since his return to serious fiction in the early 1840's. Certainly such characters as Harvey Birch and Leatherstocking had expressed a religious view of life, and *The Wept of Wish-ton-Wish* had given this theme a full, rich expression. The social aspects of Cooper's thought, however, had dominated his work in the 1830's; and, although *Home as Found* does discuss the question of democracy in moral terms, the religious theme did not generally assume major proportions again until the last of the Leatherstocking tales. Combined with the growth of this theme is the development of Cooper's view of the world as a moral chaos. The conflict of appearance and reality, developed first in *Precaution* and *The Spy* but not especially important immediately thereafter, comes into full expression in these later novels, which allow much less room for disinterested virtue than did Cooper's first work. The world darkened to Cooper's view as he grew older; and, although he is still most careful to affirm a standard of value even in the somber *Wyandotté*, it is not one that is easily found or maintained.

For Cooper never allows his characters to escape into the facile acceptance of an easy faith. Miles Wallingford's own acceptance comes as the result of the most trying circumstances when he measures himself against the forces of the universe and finds himself wanting, a process which reminds one of Leatherstocking's experience deep in the wilderness and which has much the same result. Nor does Cooper promise his believers any easy success in life. Although Miles prospers from the providential ordering of the universe, Cooper does not make his success the specific reward for his faith. Indeed, the action in these late novels would seem to imply that success in the world comes more usually from connivance with evil. Ithuel Bolt prospers as much as Miles Wallingford does, and the Willoughby family remains the classic example of the apparent injustice with which material reward is meted out in this world. Cooper was obviously as fascinated by the mystery of good and evil as Melville was later to become; and, although he never stood in open rebellion against the universe and found his affirmative value much sooner than did the later romancer, he saw it still as the profound mystery of life.

Cooper, of course, did not find so all-encompassing a symbol as did Melville for the expression of his theme, but he did manage to give it satisfying artistic form in each of these tales. The open conflict expressed in *The Two Admirals* and *The Wing-and-Wing* may at first seem too simple for many modern tastes; but, as is usual with Cooper, the surface simplicity veils a complexity beneath. The thematic relation between main and subplots in the former book and the ambiguity of its conclusion provide a depth of meaning not immediately obvious in the tale. The complex motivations of the characters in the latter book make it difficult to assign the tags of "good" or "evil" to any of them. And in *Wyandotté*, the frontier settlement—recalling as it does similar islands of civilization deep in the wilderness in *The Pioneers, The Last of the Mohicans, The Wept of Wish-ton-Wish,* and *The Deerslayer*—illustrates very well the thematic use to which Cooper could put the realistic details of his settings. In each novel, the fort or town serves a symbolic purpose that is central to the meaning of the work. The Hutted Knoll in *Wyandotté*, for instance, is as much a microcosm as are the ships in Melville or Conrad.

Finally, in *Afloat and Ashore* and *Miles Wallingford*, Cooper found an original means for developing his theme. The use of the parallel incidents on shipboard and shore gave him both narrative variety and freedom of thematic development. What happens afloat illuminates life on land, and the two together create an imaginatively convincing view of the nature of reality. His characters, like his incidents (except perhaps for the sentimentalized death of Grace), are true to life; but they also fulfill at the same time an important thematic function. As in his earliest work, Cooper was able to create in these novels a convincing background and action that form the basis for a significant moral theme. That the meaning of the action is likely to be acceptable to twentieth-century readers, who are apt to adopt as dark a view of the world as Cooper presents here, bespeaks the truth that Cooper still has something of importance to say to modern Americans. And that his themes are as well expressed through plot, setting, and character as they ever were shows unmistakably that Cooper had never really lost the artistry of his first serious fiction. Regarded in these terms, the much-neglected later novels deserve more serious consideration from modern critics than they have yet received. To be sure they are somewhat different from Cooper's early, more popular work, but they are by no means inferior.

CHAPTER *5*

The Decay of Principle

WHILE COOPER was still at work on the Miles Wallingford novels, events were taking place in New York State
that were to call him once again to more specifically social
themes. A vast acreage of land in eastern New York was
occupied by tenants under a leasehold system that dated
back to the time of the original Dutch settlement. Much of
the land was let on long-term leases, some for the duration
of a specified number of lives named in the lease, some in
perpetuity, with the payment of the rent usually to be made
in kind. Outbreaks of hostility against this so-called "feudal"
system had occurred as early as colonial times; and, by
the 1840's, relations between the two classes had degenerated
to the point of open war. Rents on the Van Rensselaer estate
were $400,000 in arrears when Stephen, the "Good Patroon,"
died in 1839; and it was soon found that they could not be
collected. The tenants, wanting to hold the land in fee, refused to pay; the landlords refused to sell on the tenants'
terms. The depressed economy of the early 1840's intensified
the trouble; and, by the time Cooper turned his full attention
to the problem, Anti-Rent Associations had been formed, the
issue had become a delicate one in state politics, and armed
bands of farmers, disguised as Indians in calico dresses and
masks, were in open rebellion.[1]

There is no denying that some of the tenants experienced
serious hardship. Even Cooper, who opposed them, allows
a good character, the Reverend Mr. Warren in *The Redskins*,
to admit that it might be better if the tenants could own the
land they farmed (p. 249). But ends do not justify the means;
and, no matter how socially desirable such a change might

have been, neither state nor Federal law could allow the open breach of contract that the tenants proposed, nor were the "Indians" within their rights when they roamed armed and disguised around the countryside. To be sure, the tenants sought justification in law for their acts: they tried to question the validity of leases confirmed by the crown before the Revolution and sought every loophole they could to give their stand a legal foundation. The problem, inevitably, became mixed with politics when the anti-rent agitators sought to destroy the landlords through special legislation enacted against them in the state legislature, and the governor himself refused to act against the "Indians" before the election of 1844 for fear of political consequences. In the face of such a social and political upheaval, a man like Cooper, who based his views on the maintenance of law and principle, could not long remain silent. He was soon in the fray with a series of novels, the Littlepage manuscripts (1845-46), that defended the landlords' position in the struggle.

I *The Littlepage Novels*

Cooper's defense, as even unsympathetic critics have admitted, was an able one,[2] based largely on the legal aspects of the problem. He pointed out in his books that the original tenant had always the option of either buying or leasing land in a country as vast and empty as the United States, that long-term leases were to the advantage of the tenant in that they insured him the use of any improvements he might make on the land, and that payment in kind was also a concession to the tenant in times when cash money was scarce. He stressed the validity of patents granted in colonial days in that they had all been confirmed by the state government after the Revolution, and he decried the idea that a tenant system was in itself undemocratic. In his view, the system could hardly be called aristocratic because the landlord had not a bit more political power than any one of his tenants. Cooper ignored, of course, the question of the tenants' hardships because he did not believe that their difficulties justified open and wholesale defiance of the law. In the legal sense, Cooper of course was right; for, as Grossman has shown, the courts eventually decided almost all the cases in favor of the landlords. But the delays of the law worked to the tenants' advantage, and most of the landlords ultimately gave up and sold their holdings (pp. 218-19).

It is a mistake, however, to see the Littlepage novels as only the expression of partisan belief in a minor and forgotten controversy, or to read them only as evidence of Cooper's withdrawal into conservatism. The books form a well-planned unit which details the social history of a part of American society through several generations; shows the inevitable changes that have taken place in American social thought; and affirms a standard of value in the landed gentry who, to Cooper's mind, were more likely to maintain a just society than the new commercial class that he had been warning his countrymen against in the fifteen years since *The Bravo*.[3] An ideal of the Christian gentleman, independent of the excitements of the hour, humble before his God, and firm in the maintenance of law and order comes through in the Little-page novels as it had in much of Cooper's work since he created the character of Judge Temple in *The Pioneers*. The Littlepage family is as much the intellectual descendant of the good Judge as the Effinghams were his actual ones; and the values Littlepages stand for are much the same as those affirmed in the Miles Wallingford novels. So regarded, the Littlepage series represents not so much a conservative re-action on Cooper's part as a further development in social terms of a moral theme that had always been a constant factor in his art.

The anti-rent struggle of the 1840's was to Cooper, there-fore, far more than an isolated instance of injustice against the landlords. It represented to him, as Spiller has shown, unmistakable evidence of the "decay of a sense of values in the American mind" (p. 306). In the three novels of the series, his intent was to trace the history of this decay of principle; and, artistically imperfect though the series may be, he succeeded admirably in detailing the degeneration he saw taking place. *Satanstoe* (1845), the first of the series, shows the founding of the estate that is to become the point of controversy when Cooper brings his story to contemporary times. But more important, it establishes a social organization out of which are to develop the attitudes of the landed class a century later. The society is rather well drawn; we see the English colonial gentry in New York in 1758, the Littlepages and the Mordaunts, both with small landed estates and with some Dutch connections. The pure Dutch are represented by the Van Valkenburghs (or Follocks, as they are called), and Albany society is presented through the highly individualized Guert Ten Eyck. On the opposite fringes of this colonial order are Major Bulstrode, a British baronet in love with Anneke Mordaunt, and Jason Newcome, a Connecticut schoolmaster.[4] All of them—including a Negro slave, Jaap, and an Onondaga Indian, Susquesus—are thrown together by the accidents of the times; they fight in Abercrombie's unsuccessful assault on Ticonderoga; and they defend both Mooseridge and Ravensnest, the Littlepage and Mordaunt patents, against the Indians.

More significant, however, are the social attitudes of the characters, which, in a sense, are both a product and a reflection of the moral positions they assume. Corny Littlepage, the hero, who, like Miles Wallingford, tells his own story, also loves Anneke Mordaunt, but so overawed is the naïve colonial by the obvious social superiority of the British aristocrat that he fears he cannot win her from a rival with so many external advantages. The major himself, in pressing his suit, counts heavily upon his wealth and title and upon the sophisticated fashions he brings from London. But so fluid has American society already become that Bulstrode makes little impression on the American girl; she dismisses all the spurious advantages he possesses in favor of the more humble, forthright, and fundamentally honest Corny. Bulstrode so greatly misinterprets the new American social order that he cannot really understand why his aristocratic advantages should count for so little, and he seeks superficial reasons to explain Corny's success (pp. 498-99). In the character of Bulstrode, therefore, the social order of privilege and power that Cooper had criticized so strongly in his European tales is banished from the series. With its dismissal, a democratic society is assured, one in which all subsequent social conflicts must develop from elements inherent in the society itself.

At first, of course, there are no serious social problems.

The only threat to the order of society and to the land patents that the Littlepage and Mordaunt families have acquired comes from the outside in the form of the French and their Huron allies, who have invaded the colony and occupy Ticonderoga. This invasion is met boldly by the characters; for, although Abercrombie is defeated, Corny and Herman Mordaunt (Anneke's father), aided by Jason, Guert, Jaap, and Susquesus, effectively defend Ravensnest and drive off the Indians. Internally, however, the society is perfectly secure. Although it has class divisions, they are by no means rigid ones. Corny can aspire to Anneke and win her though the Mordaunts are clearly the social superiors of the Littlepages; and Jason Newcome, although somewhat crude and unmannered, is accepted as at least an acquaintance. A person grossly insensitive to proper behavior, he is never snubbed by any of the characters. Indeed, Jason, clearly an intelligent man with some education, is given the opportunity to improve himself when allowed to lease on very easy terms the mill site at Ravensnest.

Much of the charm of the book derives from the obvious security of the society it describes. Only a stable social order could tolerate such festivities as the Pinkster revels or such pranks as the incident of the "Dutch treat" in Albany. In the latter event, Guert and his friends, the victims of some practical jokers who have stolen their supper, make off with one intended for the mayor—a prank which can at least be tolerated among gentlemen, but one which would have more serious meaning and consequences in a less stable social organization. Similarly, Mr. Worden, an Anglican clergyman nicknamed the "Loping Dominie" because of an incident that occurred on the river ice (pp. 170-73), could exist in no other social order. When there is no threat to the establishment, such a clergyman can be accepted affectionately for what he is: a sincere and friendly man, albeit a hedonist and coward who cares more for his own safety and a good supper than he does for the well-being of his congregation. Although he attends the cockfights and is far from being a spiritual man, he can somehow be tolerated with all his faults, for the order he represents is never called into serious question.

The appearance of Jason Newcome, however, sounds an ominous note for the future. He is the leveling democrat we first met in the person of Steadfast Dodge, the kind of left-wing Protestant that Cooper drew so well in Ithuel Bolt. Half-educated and ambitious, Jason is determined to rise in society and will use any means to achieve his end. He is the type of religionist who, while deprecating the bishops and ceremonies of the Episcopal church, will twist his own beliefs to suit his prejudices and desires; he is also the kind of democrat who continually asserts his equality with all above him. Though always obedient to the law, he knows little of principle; and, while he is fighting bravely in defense of Ravensnest, he is already scheming to get the mill site for his own. Since the Hurons have overrun the patent, he thinks it is theirs by right of conquest. When he helps drive them off, he wonders if he can't claim part of it as his own, without lease or rent, by the same right (p. 452). Jason sees everything in terms of self; he perceives no distinctions among men save those of wealth; and, unrestrained by any other principle, he seeks naturally to raise himself by the only standard he knows. His total lack of humility, his inability to perceive his own limitations, and his distorted thinking make him an obvious and serious threat to the established order.

The issue that Cooper raises in *Satanstoe*, therefore, is not so much the conflict of landlords and tenants, although he develops his material realistically in terms of that conflict. The fundamental issue is really the clash of two moral and ethical systems. On the one side—as we could expect from the earlier tales—we have the educated man, who is humble in his attainments, who accepts the inequality of men, and who thinks it no disgrace to recognize superiority in another. His pride is controlled by the stress upon humility preached in the conservative church which claims his loyalty and which forbids him to go to extremes in self-assertion. On the other side, we have the levelers, Jason and his kind, who preach equality in all things, who admit no superiority but that of money, and who are for the most part undisciplined by the "democratic" churches to which they belong. Corny, of course, in telling his story, perceives little of this (though he does begin to see through Jason). Living in a secure little world that he views with almost bright-eyed wonder, he does not perceive the changes that are already afoot. He does not foresee, for example, that the aristocratic order is on the wane, nor does he understand the seriousness of the threat to be posed by Jason's manner of thinking. He believes he is starting a dynasty of just men who will establish a secure social order for their posterity and a good life for all on their estates. But changes have already begun, the reader perceives, that will keep his dream from ever becoming a permanent reality.

In *The Chainbearer* (1845), many of the changes have already occurred a generation later in both the social and moral spheres. Socially, the new generation that has grown up during the Revolution is far more democratic. Mordaunt Littlepage, Corny's and Anneke's son, has even forgotten Bulstrode's name (p. 12) and cares nothing for what has become of him. The young have quite naturally none of the open admiration for England that their parents possessed, and they are far more likely to accept people on their inherent worth. Mordaunt, for example, who narrates the tale, is willing to accept Andries Coejemans, a wretchedly poor and not especially intelligent chainbearer, as a gentleman and an equal not only because of his position as fellow captain in his father's regiment but more particularly because of his sterling moral qualities. Mordaunt, moreover, falls in love with the Chainbearer's niece, Dus Malbone, a girl who, although born and educated a lady, is now so poor that she has had to help her uncle by carrying chain herself in his surveys. Indeed, he even believes that her experience has endowed her with qualities that make her superior to the girls of his own class whom he has passed over to win her (p. 382). In a democratic society, Mordaunt seems to believe, people are to be accepted because of worth alone and not because of possessions or inherited position. Thus far, at least, democratic change is approved in the book. The whole social order described in *Satanstoe* has been somewhat democratized.

The main issue in the book, however, is really moral. A social organization is after all but a reflection of the moral principles upon which it is based; and, since Cooper is going to the heart of the problem in these tales, he naturally stresses the moral issue involved. Thus, he insists that the kind of democracy affirmed in *The Chainbearer* is based on immutable religious principle (p. 441). Since men are fundamentally unequal, position in society should come as the reward of virtue and talent; and, once achieved, it should be accepted by the fortunate few with Christian humility and a deep submission of self to the moral laws of the universe. This concept is objectified in the person of Coejemans, the Chainbearer, whose limitations of mind and body, freely admitted, have taught him humility, and who sees no reason why he should not honor and respect those who are socially and intellectually more fortunate than he. The chains he constantly bears looped over his shoulders symbolize, therefore, both the self-imposed restraints by which he guides his life and the limits and laws by means of which society seeks to establish each man's bounds.[5] The Chainbearer, of course, as the agent of society, clearly represents the type of restraint that makes a stable social organization possible. He is Cooper's best picture of the Christian democrat.

Opposed to him is Aaron Thousandacres, the apostle of unrestrained democracy. A squatter for almost all of his seventy years, Thousandacres is the moral opposite of Chainbearer. He asserts his own will as the prime force in society, and he abhors both the physical and spiritual restraints that Coejemans marks out and accepts. He wants no law on earth or in heaven (p. 437), and he will take by brute force whatever his distorted reason tells him he needs or wants. A totally free man, he uses his freedom to satisfy his own desires; but in the process he seriously wrongs the Littlepage family, whose trees he cuts and mills on the Mooseridge patent. Thousandacres, moreover, is a product of Vermont, and Cooper presents his position as one possible result of extreme left-wing Protestantism. The squatter argues from Scriptures to support the cravings of his selfish nature; but, unrestrained by any church organization or independent clergy, he can interpret the Bible in any way he pleases to his own advantage and so find justification for his anti-social crimes. Like Ishmael Bush in *The Prairie*, whom he strongly resembles, Thousandacres represents the anarchy that would result were all restraints of principle to be removed from men.

Thousandacres and Chainbearer quite naturally come to blows in the novel, for they represent irreconcilable points of view: restraint versus license, humility versus pride, charity versus selfishness—qualities that can never be compromised. When Mordaunt Littlepage, therefore, comes to inspect the Mooseridge and Ravensnest patents after the Revolution and falls into the hands of Thousandacres, the Chainbearer—along with Jaap and Susquesus, now middle-aged men—comes quickly to his rescue. The mortal enemies confront each other in a great debate that marks the intellectual core of the novel and of the series as a whole. Neither will give an inch in his views, and it soon becomes apparent that they can never come to terms. When Chainbearer scorns an offer of marriage between his niece and the squatter's son, Thousandacres, in a moment of anger, mortally wounds the Chainbearer, only to be himself shot by Susquesus, who lies in wait in the darkness to avenge his friend. The two continue their argument until the point of death, but Chainbearer accepts his end with perfect resignation while Thousandacres struggles against the only enemy who can finally thwart him.

The truly epic struggle in which Thousandacres and Chainbearer engage in the wilderness foreshadows what is to happen in society, for the moral battle between the two is reflected in the social order as well. Once again, Jason Newcome enters the scene. Like Thousandacres, he is the product of a radical church whose theology he can interpret as he will; and he is equally self-assertive in his belief in a leveling democracy. Indeed, he may well be considered more dangerous than the squatter, for he wants respectability and all the rewards of society at the very moment he is trying to subvert the stable order. He uses the machinery of society to his own ends. He greedily bases his three-lives lease on the lives of three infants, and he bitterly complains when all three quickly die. He avoids direct connivance in Thousandacres' robbery of the Littlepages, but he is willing not only to profit from the marketing of the boards the squatter has cut but also to seek ways to cheat the squatter himself (p. 287). Worse, however, he is a respectable member of the Ravensnest community and has the demagogic power to manipulate the people to get what he wants. He succeeds, for example, in getting a majority to support the acceptance of his church in the only meetinghouse in town although only a minority are actually of his persuasion (pp. 133-41).

The selfish, greedy Jason, then, is a socialized Thousand-acres, just as Mordaunt Littlepage is a socialized Chainbearer. The issue the old men argued in the wilderness, where Cooper could present it in terms of abstract principle, will be re-fought again in society, where principle is sometimes clouded by social forms. One or the other, Cooper seems to say, must eventually prevail. Men's motivation will be either moral or economic; and, should it be the latter, an unjust, selfish society must result. Mordaunt does not yet see the danger. He himself is able to keep Jason Newcome under control; and he will not believe, as he implies some men do, that law and order will break down under the attacks of an economically motivated, unrestrained democratic opinion; he is convinced that the ordinary American's faith in principle is too strong (p. 441). In Mordaunt's lifetime, the main threat to order has been successfully met in the repulse of Thousandacres and his tribe, but the issue is clear. In the decay of principle to be traced from *Satanstoe* to *The Chainbearer,* the reader perceives an incipient threat to the social order that does not become critical until the events of the next book.

The Redskins (1846),[6] the third and last of the Littlepage novels, brings the story to 1845, the time of the anti-rent agitation; and it portrays the result of the gradual erosion of principle. The story is told by Hugh Littlepage, the grandson of Mordaunt and the son of Malbone Littlepage, who died young. He is accompanied by another Hugh, Mordaunt's second son, who goes by the name of Uncle Ro in the tale. By telescoping time in this way, Cooper takes his story forward sixty years at one leap and covers the affairs of two generations of the family at once. The novel opens in Paris, for the Littlepage family has by now become so affluent as to afford to travel for years in Europe. But although the Littlepages are wealthy, they remain, like the Effinghams, true democrats who are ever ready to defend their country's institutions. Society has changed, however, since the 1780's. The social principles professed by Aaron Thousandacres and

covertly espoused by Jason Newcome are so far in the ascend-
ancy as to have thoroughly perverted American life. As a
result, Hugh and his uncle are called home by the social
agitation these principles have caused; for Cooper portrays
the anti-rent struggle as an attempt, much akin to the squatter's, to subvert the wholesome restraints imposed by society
for the good of all.

The fundamental issue, once again, is the moral question
involved: can a society survive if fallible and selfish men can
change at will the basic principles on which the society is
based? Hugh and his uncle, in disguise on the Ravensnest
estate to learn what is afoot, regard the anti-rent "Injins"[7]
masked in calico as so many passionate men who wish to
manipulate the democratic system to their own advantage—
just as Jason Newcome would manipulate a meeting to get
the result he wanted. These leveling democrats take up
Thousandacres' cry—every man should be allowed to possess
whatever land he wants or needs—and they intimate that
none should own more than another. Since all of them, of
course, stand to gain if the estates are broken up and sold
to the tenants, Hugh and Uncle Ro consider avarice to be
their basic motivation. If their plea is allowed, Hugh argues,
it will establish the right of the majority to do as it pleases;
that is, deny at will the obligations they freely assumed. Right
and wrong would then become merely a matter of popular
vote, and demagogues could sway the masses. The minority
would soon find itself with no rights at all; for, once principle
is destroyed, it would always be at the mercy of any majority—
that is, any demagogue—that might choose to attack it.

Such is actually the situation that Hugh faces. His tenants
are aroused by demagogues, one of whom is Seneca Newcome,
Jason's descendant; and he finds even his property in church—
a canopied pew—destroyed because it offends the people's
democratic sensibilities; he also hears himself calumniated
by an anti-rent lecturer at a mass meeting presided over by
ministers of the left-wing churches. One of his barns is
burned at night and his house itself is set afire by Seneca
Newcome, all because, Hugh believes, he will not sell his
farms to the tenants on their terms. His house is even openly

attacked, toward the end of the novel, by several hundred calico "Injins."

Cooper, of course, slants his case sharply in favor of the Littlepages, but his point is a good one. Both Christian belief and civil law recognize the right of a man to his own possessions. In the face of such fundamental principle, a democratic majority can legally and morally do nothing; for a majority is not free to do as it pleases. It is only free to do right. Cooper insists, therefore, that in a democratic society, all such conflicts as that between landlord and tenant should be referred to principle. To decide the issue in any other way is merely to give the advantage to numbers—and they are more often wrong in their opinion than otherwise.

To oppose the tenants' view, Cooper imports a band of real Indians from the prairies to affirm the proper values. Jaap and Susquesus, both well over a hundred, are still alive as tangible links with the past; and the Indian, long called the Upright Onondaga, provides the final affirmative note in the book. The prairie Indians have sought him out not only because of his great age but also because of the example of self-command that he long before had set for his tribe. The whites have long known that there was a remarkable story in the Indian's past, but only now is it revealed to them that his great accomplishment was submission to tribal law when his own bent and the majority of the tribe would have condoned his breaking it. He gave up his love for an Indian girl because by the laws of the tribe she belonged to the brave who had captured her. The Indian's assertion of the principle of self-restraint under generally agreed rules points up the selfish, undisciplined spirit of the tenants; but his presence also is a living rebuke to all white men that the land they squabble over was originally wrenched from the grievously wronged red men. In the face of such virtue, the calico "Injins" melt away.

This conclusion, of course, does not quite come off as Cooper had hoped; for, although it makes his point well, it does such violence to the realities of his tale that it is difficult to accept artistically. Nor is this the only flaw in the book. Too much is argued; too little is dramatized for it to succeed as a novel, for the characters endlessly discuss the relative merits of the various points in the controversy. To a certain extent, of course, some of this discussion, as well as Hugh's violent and belligerent tone, can be justified by the point of view of the tale. One can well understand that the land-lords would sometimes assume this tone and discuss at length material that would have been of consuming interest to them. We expect Hugh and Uncle Ro to be strong in their belief; but Cooper does not keep his material sufficiently under control, as he did in *Satanstoe* and *The Chainbearer;* he turns his book, therefore, into a wordy exercise in polemics. *The Redskins* is certainly not so bad as many critics have inti-mated—Brady, for example, is quite right in defending it (p. 80)—but Cooper made in it the same mistake he always committed when criticizing the contemporary scene. Unable to achieve sufficient detachment from it, he failed in *The Redskins* for the reason he failed in *Home as Found*: he was himself too emotionally involved.

The Redskins, therefore, does not compare with either *Satanstoe* or *The Chainbearer* as a work of fiction. Cooper could not hope to achieve with the contemporary scene the same full-bodied picture of a social order that he had de-scribed in *Satanstoe;* nor, once having objectified his theme so well in the conflict between Chainbearer and Thousand-acres, could he find an equally satisfactory means for present-ing it in the succeeding novel. Nevertheless, in the characters of the aged Indian and of the Negro, he managed to find a pair of symbols that almost save his book and that certainly give a unity and coherence to the series that it would not otherwise possess.[8] Both Jaap and Susquesus, the one a slave who fulfilled himself in slavery through loyal service to his masters, the other an Indian who achieved a remarkable triumph of self-discipline, stand as living links with tradition and as living symbols of the ideal of submission of self to a higher principle that marks the affirmative value in the series. Regarded in these terms, *The Redskins*—for all its faults—remains a significant achievement; for, although it is clearly weaker than either of the tales that preceded it, it performs an important function in bringing the series as a whole to its proper conclusion.

II *The Crater*

That Cooper himself was somewhat dissatisfied with the effect he had achieved in *The Redskins* seems obvious enough, for more than once he pauses in the course of the narrative to apologize for the harshness of Hugh's tone (pp. 133, 535). That he was also aware of the reason for his failure seems equally evident, for in the next year he published *The Crater* (1847), a tale which develops a similar theme by means of a plot and setting totally removed from the contemporary struggle. Indeed, in laying the scene in the South Sea islands and in presenting the material through an imaginary society, Cooper seems to have consciously sought to make his meaning as clear—and as acceptable—to a contemporary audience as he possibly could. Thus, although on the surface *The Crater* is developed as a tale of adventure and the social criticism appears only in the last thirty pages of the book, the theme itself is the same as that of the Littlepage series: the decay that occurs in society when the moral purpose that gave it life has been lost.[9] In *The Crater*, the theme is presented more compactly than in the previous books; for the rise and fall of the society is compressed into the space of a single volume.[10]

The first half of the novel is concerned with the founding of the Utopian colony. Mark Woolston, the young first mate of an American vessel, is shipwrecked with a lone companion on a reef in mid-Pacific. Fortunately, the ship is not destroyed; and, like another Crusoe,[11] Mark, with Bob Betts, a seaman, manages to plant some seeds in the volcanic ash of the island and to build a pinnace in which to return to America. Bob and the pinnace, however, are washed away in a storm, and Mark is left alone on the island, much as Miles Wallingford was on his raft in the Atlantic. Like Wallingford, too, Mark learns a serious lesson in his solitude—one which stands him in good stead in the future. A man of considerable intelligence and knowledge, he studies the sea and sky around him; gazing at the stars at night, he speculates about his own helplessness in the face of the vast expanse of emptiness that surrounds him. He seeks and finds his God in the harmony of the starlit universe that arches above him, and he perceives his own insufficiency to satisfy his most rudimentary wants should Providence fail to smile on him.

Mark's lesson is made complete one night when a sudden earthquake raises his islands above the water; he not only comes to feel the immense power of God revealed in nature, but also finds himself the possessor of a whole new creation, including a lovely tropical island raised to mountain heights. Like Adam in Paradise—and Cooper's diction justifies the comparison[12]—Mark has a new world to do with as he pleases. Thus, when Betts at last returns with relatives and friends of both men, they promptly start a new colony with Mark at its head. Governor Woolston, a man of deep knowledge and sincere faith—the result of his early education and of his experience alone on the reef—is therefore pictured as the proper kind of leader for a democratic society. The moral principles he has derived from his training and experience serve as the basis for the new social organization: a just society where all men have equal rights but where only the most virtuous and talented rule. The rest submit in humility to the reign of law, just as the governor humbly acquiesces to the law of God as revealed in the Christian religion. Cooper has clearly gone out of his way to stress the moral foundation that must be laid before any lasting society can be formed.

But Cooper's purpose is only partly fulfilled in the description of the Utopian colony, for no sooner has he pictured a rich and flourishing country than he deliberately sets about its destruction. As the colony grows in numbers and in wealth and as new colonists are admitted, the people begin to lose the humility they had once possessed. They come to believe that they are the cause of their own good fortune and that they deserve the good things that have come to them (pp. 462-63). New elements enter the land in the form of a newspaper editor, lawyers, and wrangling ministers, imported by people who were not satisfied with the single Episcopalian Mark had provided. None of these men has ever been impressed, as Mark has been, with his own insignificance; none has developed the necessary spirit of humility. Like Thousand-acres and the calico "Injins," they begin to entertain the mistaken notion that they, the people, are sovereign in all things. The editor asserts that the majority is free to do whatever it pleases, the lawyers and merchants desert principle for gain, and the rival ministers cause endless dissension with their arguments about the externals of religion. All subordination is lost; principle disappears at the whim of the majority; and the people fall under the power of demagogues who seek only personal gain.

Mark is robbed of both his property and his office in a carefully manipulated election, and he leaves his decaying colony in disgust to visit his home in America. When he returns nine months later, he learns that a second earthquake has drowned his islands, and he views the disaster as the judgment of God upon a society that has deserted sound principle for gratification of material desires. A society cannot survive when its moral basis is lost, Cooper argues; and this belief he symbolizes dramatically in the physical destruction of the colony. Cooper obviously intends *The Crater* to be a parable of the United States, which had once been a similar earthly paradise in which just principles of government had been established. With the degeneration of his Utopian colony, he seeks, therefore, to warn his countrymen of a similar decay in contemporary American society. The theme of *The Crater* is precisely the same as that of the Littlepage series and it carries the same warning to the American people. Unless they return to a belief in principle and submit in Christian humility to the rule of law, they cannot expect their society long to endure.

But although *The Crater* is the sharpest presentation of Cooper's mature social theory, it is by no means so artistically satisfactory as the preceding novels. It lacks the objective density of the Littlepage tales; it underlines its theme too obviously in the depiction of the Utopian society. Where the Littlepage series describes a gradual shift in attitude over a hundred-year period, *The Crater* tries to telescope the material into the span of a single life. Inevitably, the book has a sketchy quality. The incidents are far too briefly drawn and the characters are not sufficiently rounded. Mark has little of the individuality of the three Littlepage heroes, and there are no minor characters to equal the many excellent ones in all three Littlepage tales. *The Crater* must be considered, therefore, an interesting literary document: it is important historically as the first American Utopia, and it is significant intellectually because it provides so clear a presentation of Cooper's mature conclusions about the relation of social forms to the moral concepts that lie beneath them. As a work of art, however, it is one of his less successful works; it is akin in its theme-ridden plot to *The Redskins* and the social tales of the 1830's.

III   *Loss of Values*

Despite their faults, both the Littlepage novels and *The Crater* mark an important climax in Cooper's career: in these books he managed to unite the major moral and social themes that had been in his work from the beginning and to define their relation to each other more precisely than he had yet done. In a sense, his major work was over. Never again was he to present such sweeping studies of the nature of society, its moral basis, and its current decay. Instead, in his four remaining novels, he turned to more specific studies of the loss of value in American life in order to analyze the cause and present the cure as he had come to see it. These four novels are a miscellaneous group whose themes are developed through the use of a variety of materials: the sea, the forest, and contemporary American society. Without exception, however, they all deal with one aspect or another of the decay of principle. *Jack Tier, The Sea Lions,* and *The Ways of the Hour*—all treat the various human failings of greed, selfishness, or pride that afflict undisciplined men and lead them astray. *The Oak Openings* and *The Sea Lions* also affirm most specifically the standard of Christian values that Cooper increasingly saw as the only possible means for controlling erring men. The books are diverse in subject matter and somewhat unsuccessful in treatment, but all point unmistakably to the same conclusion.

Jack Tier (1848), usually dismissed as merely a realistic—and inferior—reworking of *The Red Rover,* has received little careful analysis. Yet despite its obvious relation to this earlier tale—Cooper closely parallels the characters and incidents in the two books[13]—*Jack Tier* has much to say about the decline of value in modern life. One of the very few of his sea tales to take place in contemporary times, the novel clearly intimates that the decay has proceeded so far that service afloat, always with Cooper an occupation that draws upon the finest principles of loyalty and duty, has degenerated into an endless pursuit of gain.[14] Captain Heidegger of *The Red Rover* had been an outlaw for patriotic reasons, but Stephen Spike, the captain of the *Swash* in *Jack Tier*, traffics with the enemy during the Mexican War and becomes a traitor for pay. The Rover was a generous and considerate gentleman to the ladies who fell into his power; Spike is a coarse and greedy lecher who abandoned his wife for another woman and who now pursues the young and innocent Rose Budd. He has, in fact, spent his life in the pursuit of women and gold. Utterly devoid of faith in anything but sensuous gratification, Spike has sacrificed all "principles and duty to the narrow interests of the moment," and he finds it impossible even on his deathbed to pray to the God he had so long neglected (p. 503).

Stephen Spike, however, is only an ordinary sinner, coarse and gross in his evil. More dangerous, because more respectable, is the type of modern character represented by Mrs. Budd, Rose's aunt. This woman represents to a great extent the person of average or less ability who, utterly devoid of humility, takes great pride in a knowledge she does not possess. Through her conceited ignorance, she causes endless trouble in the book. She has absorbed a smattering of nautical knowledge from her late husband, but she has confused her facts and language so badly that she is no longer able to make much sense. Nevertheless, she goes blithely on her way, refusing to be corrected or to accept the word of those who know better than she. Worse, she sometimes acts upon her knowledge, as when she loses the *Swash's* boat by her officious attempt to retie the painter which she believes poorly secured (p. 237). The easy dupe of the unscrupulous Spike, she leads her niece into his clutches because of her inability to penetrate the truth, nor does she learn the nature of Spike's true character until her last moments, when, trying to lighten an overloaded yawl in the surf, Spike casts her bodily from the ship and orders her hands cut off when she hangs on for dear life.

Mrs. Budd's failure is clearly the result of an ignorance

which, aggressive in its conceit, cannot admit its own liability to error. Equally dangerous, however, is the capable knowledge that becomes too proud for faith. To a certain extent, Harry Mulford, Spike's first mate of the *Swash*, represents the latter attitude. Although thoroughly honest himself and unconscious of Spike's treachery, Mulford allows himself to be governed by loyalty to his ship and love for Rose Budd. Only when· he finds himself and Rose in the direst straits, afloat on the bottom of a capsized schooner near the Florida reef, does he humble "his pride of profession and of manhood" in a prayer to the God he had not sought since he joined the *Swash* (pp. 254-55). Like Miles Wallingford and Mark Woolston, therefore, Harry Mulford is brought to his knees only by the most terrible circumstances. By no means so evil as Spike and certainly more rational than Mrs. Budd, he is nonetheless in danger of serious error until he perceives his own insufficiency to achieve the ends he desires. Full of pride in his abilities, Mulford represents the neglect of the wholesome humility that Cooper insists is the necessary foundation for the good life.

Two of these characters, Stephen Spike and Mrs. Budd, are the primary motivating forces in the novel; and, since their actions are governed by willful greed and gross ignorance, the result is disaster. But Cooper does not ignore the function of good; for Señor Montefalderon, the Mexican agent, is motivated by forces as pure as those that animated Harvey Birch; Harry Mulford is made at last to see his error in relying so much upon himself. Moreover, the United States Navy is always in pursuit of the *Swash* to reimpose the order that Stephen Spike has defied. Yet much of the damage that Mrs. Budd and Captain Spike cause is irretrievable. Mrs. Budd, for example, not only goes to her death, but takes her faithful maid, Biddy Noon, with her. And the effects of the gross evil that Spike himself has created are well symbolized in the person of Jack Tier, who is really Spike's wife, Mary Swash, in disguise. Cooper had used disguised women before in his romantic tales; but, in contrast to the handsome young women masquerading as men in *The Red Rover* and *The Water-Witch,* Jack is a fat and ugly tar, completely unsexed by the twenty years' struggle during which she has worked her way from ship to ship in search of the man who had deserted her on an island while he went in pursuit of another woman. Cooper, moreover, allows her no romantic triumph; for, when Spike on his deathbed finally realizes who she is, he turns away from her with a groan of disgust at what she has become. In deep bitterness of spirit, Jack can only turn away and weep (p. 495).

Jack Tier, therefore, represents something far more serious than the mere realistic reworking of a romantic tale. It is a rather grim but essentially true criticism of a world where all sense of principle has been lost. In such a world—by implication, contemporary American society—all value is subordinated to money; treason becomes merely another profitable business; and men like Spike simply take what they want, whatever the consequences. In addition, Spike's assertion of self in his villainous actions has its counterpart in the character of Mrs. Budd, who is only a fool in her arrogance and pride, but a dangerous fool because she is free to act and does not recognize her folly. Even in Mulford we find a touch of the modern disease of pride and self-assurance in his accomplishments. Throughout the book, also, superstition and ignorance, always twins in Cooper's view, are everywhere apparent (pp. 410-11, 419). To be sure, Cooper does not allow his book to come to a completely somber end. Mulford and Rose marry and retrieve Jack Tier to the ways of feminine civilization. But the dominant tone is a grim one, for Cooper posits a world where coherence and order have been lost in the only standard of value that many will admit—monetary gain.

Such a view, of course, was by no means new with Cooper, for one can trace it back to the character of Mr. Wharton in *The Spy*, through the social criticism of the 1830's, to the Newcome clan of the Littlepage series. But not since *Wyandotté* had Cooper come so close to giving the world over to material greed. Nor was his solution to the problem—the religious view—at all unusual, for this too had always been a constant factor in his work. Nonetheless, when Cooper did turn to the affirmation of religious values in succeeding novels, he not only stressed them far more strongly than he ever had before, but also presented them in more strictly Christian terms. Thus, *The Oak Openings* (1848), Cooper's last Indian tale, resembles both *The Wept of Wish-ton-Wish* and *The Deerslayer* in its deeply Christian meaning, but it goes much farther than either of them in the explicit development of the concept. Although much of the story is taken up with the staple flight and pursuit of Cooper's frontier fiction, this adventurous element is at last subordinated to the fundamentally religious theme.

The plot itself is simple. In a sudden British and Indian assault, Mackinaw, Chicago, and Detroit quickly fall to the enemy; and a group of Americans and their Indian friend, Pigeonswing, are isolated in Western Michigan. These characters become involved with an Indian chief who seems to belong to no tribe; Scalping Peter, a kind of combined Tecumseh and Prophet, wants, like Magua and Mahtoree in earlier books, to unite the tribes to destroy the white men. The whites—Le Bourdon (Ben Boden), a bee hunter; Gershom Waring, his wife, and sister—fall into Peter's hands when he arrives to preside over a meeting of the tribes. With him are Parson Amen, a Methodist missionary, and Corporal Flint, a survivor of the attack on Chicago, both of whom are unaware of Peter's real motives and trust him implicitly. The close proximity of Indians and whites among the Openings gives Cooper the opportunity to make some telling intellectual and moral contrasts. The superstition of the Indians is balanced by the knowledge and skill of the whites, especially Le Bourdon, who dupes them twice with pretended magic. The dignity and sobriety of Peter are contrasted with the bestial drunkenness of Waring, and the deep faith of the minister is set against the warlike spirit of the soldier who places his faith in physical force.

The central conflict of the book, however, is between Scalping Peter and Parson Amen; everything that happens is triggered by their relation, and they contribute most to the novel's meaning. The parson is a religious enthusiast. A man of little education but great religious zeal, he has become obsessed with the idea that the Indian nations are really the descendants of the lost tribes of Israel, and he reads his Old Testament as if it made a specific prophecy both of the tribes he sees before him and of Scalping Peter himself.

From one point of view, therefore, Parson Amen is akin to Mrs. Budd in *Jack Tier*, for his uninstructed ignorance, like hers, leads him and his companions into serious difficulties that result in his death. But unlike the widow, the minister is a devout Christian whose behavior at the moment of his gravest trial redeems him and all his errors. Once aware of the truth—that the Indians who have pretended to be his friends are about to kill him—he obeys the Christian injunction and prays for his enemies with his dying breath. Parson Amen thus becomes a saint and martyr, a type of the crucified Christ, in his death.[15] Indeed, as Grossman has observed (p. 230), he even shows the share in the universal guilt possessed by the Indians who, although shocked when they learn that the white men had killed the Son of God, do much the same thing when they murder the saintly parson.

More important, however, is the effect on Peter, who begins as a persecutor of the whites and ends their friend. Once their implacable foe, Peter is first softened by Margery Waring, who tells him that she admits the justice of the Indians' grievances. He refuses to be influenced by Parson Amen, however, partly because he cannot accept the good man's theories on the lost tribes, but most particularly because he cannot believe that any man would willingly forgive those who had hurt him. In an obvious echo of the words of St. Thomas the Apostle, Peter frankly states: "I shall not believe that any do this, till I see it" (p. 384). When he does witness the parson's exemplary death, he is suddenly struck, therefore, by the truth of the man's belief; and, like another persecutor (Paul on the road to Damascus), he experiences a remarkable conversion. In language highly evocative of the Christian tradition, Peter becomes as a little child (p. 427) and puts on the new man. "I am no longer Peter—I must be another Injin" (p. 428). In the light of such evidence, we are certainly justified in reading a special significance as well into the name Peter and seeing the relation of Parson and Indian as a symbolic representation of the repeated effects of the sacrifice on Calvary.

Up to this point, *The Oak Openings* is a powerful book because of the strength of its Christian statement; but Cooper, unfortunately, could not bring his tale to a satisfactory end.

He hurries his characters off the scene in a rather anticlimactic fashion and attempts to make a contemporary application of the theme in an unsuccessful coda appended to the novel. Setting the conclusion in 1848, Cooper allows the aged Peter to lecture the reader about the need for Christian principles to influence all men in much the same way they animate the social order now developing on Prairie Round. This ending, of course, is a dreadful mistake, for the idyllic view of rural Michigan does not ring true. Too much of what Cooper had recently written had stressed convincingly the utter decay of principle in the modern world; the affirmation seems, therefore, contrived when presented in terms of a contemporary social order. Besides, the powerful Christian meaning of the body of the novel demanded a stronger conclusion than the celebration of rural virtues and a pious sermon by Peter. Intellectually, Cooper's purpose is clear: he wants to stress his belief that the progress of American society must be seen in Christian terms if it is to yield any worthwhile results. But the bald statement of this ideal mars irretrievably the overwhelming effect he had achieved in the central part of the book.

Similar criticism can be leveled against *The Sea Lions* (1849), which presents so specific an affirmation of Christian values that many critics have dismissed the book as merely a Trinitarian tract.[16] There is some justice in their objections: Cooper does ride his thesis hard; and he includes a prosy character, Stimson, who makes the properly orthodox comment at each moment of danger. And yet *The Sea Lions* develops a much more general theme than such criticism seems to imply, for Roswell Gardiner's return to Christian orthodoxy as a result of his experience in the antarctic is not the total meaning of the tale. Rather, Cooper is once again describing the erosion of principle in modern American society, and he illustrates the decay in at least two important areas. From one point of view, *The Sea Lions*, like *Jack Tier*, is a well-developed study in human greed; for every important incident in the book is motivated by the avarice of one of the principal characters. From another, it is a study of intellectual arrogance of the type that Cooper had criticized as early as his caricature of Dr. Bat, the physical scientist, in *The Prairie*. That Cooper did not manage to weld these two parts sufficiently marks his true artistic failure in the book.

Cooper's picture of human greed is convincingly done. Deacon Pratt, the good church member who conceals from a sailor's heirs the whereabouts of some seal islands and buried pirate treasure, is a well-drawn character. The deacon's greed for the wealth he does not need sends Roswell on his antarctic adventure; the avarice of the sailor's heir, Captain Daggett, who follows Gardiner to learn the location of the treasures, is instrumental in trapping both himself and Gardiner on the seal islands throughout the long antarctic winter. Cooper's most telling attack on cupidity, however, ocurs toward the end of the tale when Deacon Pratt, having long given up the voyage as lost, is already on his deathbed; and his friends and relatives, motivated by avarice, have gathered around him in an attempt to pry him loose from some of his possessions. Even the minister of his church, Parson Whittle, makes broad hints to his dying parishioner that he bequeath his wealth to the church (pp. 460-61). Although all are acting badly, the deacon is worst of all; for, when Gardiner, just back from his harrowing experience, comes into the sick room, Deacon Pratt can think of nothing but his possessions and dies clutching the bag of pirate gold that Gardiner has brought. Like Captain Spike in *Jack Tier*, the deacon—and most of his neighbors—is tireless in pursuit of money.

But if Cooper is criticizing the materialism of modern Americans in these characters, he does not consider this fault the most serious one. Although they worship a golden idol, there is, in his opinion, an idolatry worse than that— one which is in a sense the fundamental cause of all other evils. This error is illustrated in the character of Roswell Gardiner, who, although generally honest enough, is a free-thinker. Strongly influenced by the Deists, he believes only what his own reason can understand. He refuses to accept the Christian mystery of the incarnation because it seems improbable to him that God would submit himself to be crucified. Lacking the faith and humility of Mary Pratt, the deacon's niece whom he loves, Roswell makes his own mind the standard by which all things are judged. Totally without faith, he rejects whatever is beyond his power of thought. Thus, although Cooper places the issue in terms of Trinitarian theology, his theme concerns something much more general than one article of dogma. He attacks the whole rationalist attitude that would make the human mind sufficient to itself in all things. The danger inherent in such a belief he had already well illustrated in the character of Mrs. Budd, and he saw it also as the cause of much of the failure of democratic society where men refuse to admit their individual or collective liability to error. This attitude is fundamental also to all the sins of human selfishness which elevate the wishes of the individual above all other considerations.

Thus, although Gardiner is a man of considerable knowledge and skill, pride in his abilities sometimes gets him into serious difficulty, as when he almost goes aground off the coast of North Carolina because he wants to show he can stay on his course as long as Daggett can (p. 146). Indeed, it is not until he braves the terrible cold of the antarctic winter that he learns the humility he needs. Forced to an existence on the barest level of survival with his fuel running low and the bitter winter not yet past, Gardiner, like Mark Woolston, comes to perceive his own smallness in the face of God's immensity, his weakness before His power. He realizes, therefore, how presumptuous he has been to demand that his God be one that he can understand. In his newly found humility, he realizes how much is beyond both his abilities and his understanding, even in the physical world where so much is under man's influence if not actually subject to his control. With this perception come both faith in what is beyond him and a realization that his limited powers cannot pick and choose among Christian doctrines for those that he wishes to believe. "In this frame of mind Roswell was made to see that Christianity admitted of no half-way belief; it was all true, or it was wholly false" (p. 411). He submits his intelligence and will to those elements that are a mystery to him and is converted to Trinitarian belief.

Gardiner's conversion, unfortunately, is not so convincingly shown as was Scalping Peter's in *The Oak Openings,* and

Cooper made the mistake of repeating a device—the human being alone confronting the violent power of nature—that he had already used to the same end in *Miles Wallingford* and *The Crater*. Yet despite its artistic deficiencies, *The Sea Lions* remains an interesting book in its clear statement of Cooper's belief in the almost complete loss of value in national life. The worship of gold has gone so far as to infect even those who are the avowed members of a Christian church —even the minister himself. Besides, what has not been corrupted by the curse of materialism has been touched by that of infidelity in those who, possessing a little knowledge, would make the worship of their own minds their primary purpose in life. Cooper is clearly attacking here, as he did in both the Littlepage novels and *The Crater*, two elements that he saw increasing in American society—the worship of material goods and the naïve faith in human reason—that marked the decay of principle, the loss of the old humility that, in all of his gentleman heroes since Judge Temple, had sought other articles of faith than gold and that was always willing to admit that there were mysteries beyond the power of human understanding, areas to which the unaided human mind could never penetrate.

So important was the latter concept in Cooper's view that he devoted the whole of his last book, *The Ways of the Hour* (1850), to an exposition of the limitations of the human mind.[17] To present his theme, Cooper selected a subject that was well adapted to his purpose—a trial by jury in a capital case. A jury trial is after all an exercise in human reason, for it is based upon the faith that twelve ordinary citizens can determine the truth from an examination of the evidence. And trial for a capital offense is a serious matter, for the life of a human being is forfeit if the jury should err. Cooper, of course, slants his material strongly against the jury system by detailing the many tricks lawyers have used to select favorable jurors and to influence the rest unduly. He clearly shows how public opinion can be stirred up by hired agents or by a partisan press to the detriment of one side of the case, and he attacks the newly adopted system of electing judges by popular vote, for the men who are chosen are thereby brought under the influence of popular pressure if they hope to be re-elected. Cooper constructs a persuasive case against trial by jury in a democratic society, but this attack is incidental to his central purpose.

The Ways of the Hour is far more than an exposé of contemporary social evils. For besides the many corrupt practices, Cooper saw operating some fundamental principles that account for the decay he perceived in American society. Basically, an unrestrained democracy must place its faith in the fundamental honesty, impartiality, and rationality of the common man—qualities that Cooper did not believe could be expected from the mass of the people. He thought, therefore, that such a society was laying its foundations on faulty premises. It was not that men are willfully evil; for, by and large, they mean well. But although most intend to be honest and truthful, few are at all aware of the subtle rationalizations by which they distort conclusions and corrupt themselves.

In the case of Mary Monson, Cooper presents in *The Ways of the Hour* a rich stranger in a small town, who is suspected of murdering and robbing an old couple with whom she has been living and of burning their house. Two bodies are found, which, though reduced to charred skeletons, are assumed to be the remains of Peter Goodwin and his wife. Besides, Mrs. Goodwin's hoard of gold is missing; and an old German woman, said to have been living there, is not to be found. The case against Mary Monson is damaging but not conclusive, and Cooper presents the matter as one of honest doubt.

He does not, however, reveal the truth at once. To maintain suspense and to convince the reader of the truth of his theme, Cooper refrains from giving him any more information than the jurors themselves possess at any given time. Nothing is known of Mary Monson's past; and the jurors, along with her own lawyers, have to decide on her guilt or innocence solely on the basis of the evidence presented. Such a conclusion, Cooper seems to say, is extremely difficult to reach, for many factors affect perception of the truth. We believe what we expect to be true; hence, the townspeople and most of the doctors believe that the corpses are the remains of the Goodwins. We rely heavily on the opinion of numbers; hence, the jurors believe the evidence of five doctors concerning the sex of the skeletons though one doctor believes correctly that both are female. We accept the testimony of a well-known witness of good reputation, though she turns out to have been lying. Indeed, so difficult is it to perceive the truth that even the best-educated and most intelligent of men find it hard to penetrate Mary Monson's motives; and Dunscomb, her lawyer, vacillates between belief in her guilt and innocence. How much harder is it, therefore, for the average man, not especially intelligent and poorly schooled, to arrive at a just verdict?

Indeed, Mary herself adds to the confusion by spreading false rumors around the town in her own behalf and by concealing evidence in her favor because she is obsessed with the idea that the state's evidence alone should clear her. As one would expect, the whole system of justice collapses under the strain. Tried first for the murder of Peter Goodwin, Mary is found guilty by the jury and sentenced to die; but Peter turns up alive. Mary has thus been convicted of a murder that has not been committed, and the jury has shown itself unable to arrive at a just decision when an error would have most serious consequences. Mary finally takes her defense into her own hands, and gradually the truth is revealed. The trusted witness lied because she had stolen the gold, and the deaths of the two women and the fire are shown to have been accidents. But as we watch Mary operate toward the close of the novel, we begin to see that she is herself far from sane. The truth is thus finally revealed by a mad woman, a truth that honest and well-intentioned men could not discern by means of their rational faculties. The whole machinery of justice is completely frustrated by the inability of ordinary men to penetrate to the truth.

The Ways of the Hour is thus by far the most damaging of Cooper's attacks on American society, for the whole social organization described in the book dissolves into a kind of chaotic madness. Hopelessly perverted by the weakness of the common man, the system of justice is defeated in a triumph of unreason. This attack is, of course, consistent with the ones he had been waging for many years; and it reveals once more Cooper's belief that principle was being lost in American society. Guilt and innocence, justice and truth, Cooper seems to say, are not qualities to be determined by a vote of the majority. They are absolute principles above the cavils of opinion and must be determined on some other basis. The government of the universe, Dunscomb observes in the novel, is not democratic (p. 309). All truth and justice derive from God, upon whom the seeker must ultimately depend if he hopes to discern the truth (p. 498). Only to the extent that fallible men are willing to admit with humility their liability to error will they ever be able to find the truth and make it the basis of a just social order. *The Ways of the Hour* complements, therefore, *The Redskins* and the close of *The Crater* by showing the ends toward which the loss of principle is driving American society.

But if *The Ways of the Hour* is closely related in theme to Cooper's other late novels of social criticism, it is superior to them in both conception and execution. The use of a murder trial as the unifying element in the tale was a happy invention, for it allowed him to develop his theme through the use of material admirably suited to his purpose. At one stroke, he could portray both the abuses that had crept into the administration of justice and the fundamental reason for their presence. He was able to show the fallibility of the human mind in an area where right and wrong may be clearly distinguished and to suggest the madness of the belief that a just and stable society can exist without the proper subordination of the mass of men to those possessing superior virtue and knowledge. The book, of course, has its faults: the trial itself is somewhat clumsily handled, and Cooper could not resist the temptation to lecture his readers on specific contemporary problems. In form, however, *The Ways of the Hour* is as vigorous and interesting an experiment as were any of his American tales of the early 1820's; and the theme is presented with an intellectual vitality that we come to associate with Cooper even when he is not writing at his best.

Indeed, all of Cooper's late work is marked by an astonishing vigor. For all their faults—and only the first two Littlepage novels may be considered among his best work—the tales show no sign of intellectual or artistic fatigue. Cooper's late works are especially significant for the strength and

clarity of their intellectual statement. For thirty years, he
had pondered deeply about the possibilities and realities of
life in America. At times he had been at open war with his
countrymen and had satirized them harshly, but he had always remained the deeply concerned patriot who wished
to see the United States fulfill its promise. Now at the end
of his life, still ready to do battle for what he believed in,
as in the anti-rent struggle, he tried to show his fellow
citizens the areas wherein the greatest danger to American
democracy lay. Thoroughly committed still to the democratic
form of government, he tried to demonstrate the evils inherent
in a form of society that placed no value on any pre-eminence
save that derived from accumulated wealth, that saw no
need for humility in the mass of free men. He became, of
course, more explicitly religious in his themes as the years wore
on; but this shift implies not so much a change in attitude
as an increased emphasis upon a standard of value that in one
form or another had always been affirmed in his works.

Artistically, too, Cooper's late novels are of considerable
interest. Despite the serious lapses apparent in several of them,
we leave his final tales with a deep respect for the remarkable
inventive powers of the man. The use of the Littlepage
family in the anti-rent novels, the rise and fall of the Utopian
society in *The Crater,* the sacrificial death of Parson Amen
in *The Oak Openings,* the antarctic voyage in *The Sea Lions*—
all of these are, with the murder trial in *The Ways of the
Hour,* truly original conceptions; and each is well suited to
the theme he wished to express. To the end he was able
to generate a significant moral theme from the realities of
the environment in which his characters move, a theme that
can be fully understood only if one perceives the moral drama
expressed through the physical action. Only rarely, of course,
in his late works—perhaps in *Satanstoe* and *The Chainbearer*
alone—does Cooper fully achieve the kind of interplay of
characters in setting and action that yields his best results.
Nonetheless, his relative success in such other works as *Jack
Tier, The Oak Openings,* and *The Ways of the Hour* clearly
demonstrates that Cooper never completely lost his fine
artistic gifts. Even his partial failures bear the unmistakable
stamp of his great and unfailing talent.

CHAPTER 6

A General Estimate

WITH THE PUBLICATION of *The Ways of the Hour,* Cooper's significant work was done. To be sure, his unsuccessful play, *Upside Down, or Philosophy in Petticoats* (1850), was yet to be performed,[1] and several fugitive pieces were still to appear.[2] These are, however, rather slight productions which, hardly worthy of serious criticism, may be passed over in silence. His final book, a history of New York called *The Towns of Manhattan,* on which he was working when he died in September, 1851, survives as only a fragment; for most of the manuscript was destroyed in a fire after his death.[3] At mid-century, therefore, just as American literature was about to achieve its first great flowering, Cooper completed his thirty years of novel-writing and general social criticism. His performance was a remarkable one. To look back upon the bulk of his work from the perspective of the intervening century is to be impressed with its vigor, its honesty, and its essential unity; for Cooper's work is very much of a piece. Although at first glance there appears to be a great disparity between the American tales of the 1820's and the social criticism which followed and between the dark novels of the 1840's and the Littlepage series that succeeded them, all are seen to be closely related when viewed in terms of the broad vision of life that Cooper consistently developed in his work.

Thus, although the general criticism of Cooper tends to stress the apparent dichotomy in his thought revealed, it is said, by the Leatherstocking tales and the Littlepage novels, actually even these seemingly diverse works are, as Brady has correctly observed (p. 78), much more alike in their themes

than has generally been admitted. To perceive their basic
similarity, however, we must understand their intellectual
background. Fundamental to Cooper's work is a moral view
of the world and of men that has its social aspects, to be sure,
but which is basically concerned with man's relation first
to the God revealed in the order of nature and only then
to his fellows in an ordered society. Seen in these terms, the
moral tales of forest and sea have a general social significance
in that they establish the standards for men to follow in a
social relation; and the social theories that Cooper presents
throughout his career are completely intelligible to contemporary readers only if seen in relation to the moral concepts that in Cooper's view form the basis for all social organizations. Even the supposed contradictions in Cooper's
political thought—represented, some critics believe, by his
European tales of the 1830's and the criticism of American life
that followed—are easily reconciled when we finally perceive
the moral view that formed the basis for his criticism of both
the aristocratic and democratic systems. It is important,
therefore, in our final estimate of Cooper, to review his
work as a whole in order to observe the consistency of his
intellectual position and the place of his various novels in its
general exposition.

For example, basic themes recur throughout his fiction.
From the very beginning in *The Spy*, Cooper draws a picture
of the loss of order in society and the moral confusion that
results, a theme he was to present again in such works as
The Two Admirals and *Wyandotté*. Without the proper principle of subordination working throughout society, man loses
his ability to make intelligent choices and to act on the basis
of principle. In many of his characters, Cooper clearly illustrates the dangers that are always incurred when order
is destroyed. People turn to other principles upon which to
base their decisions. Mr. Wharton, like Joel Strides, substitutes material wealth for the fundamental principles of loyalty
and right which should provide the proper standard of conduct; Admiral Bluewater and Captain Willoughby come to
such an impasse that for each free choice of a course of
action becomes all but impossible. Some succeed, like Willoughby's son, in manipulating society for their own ends;

others, like Sir Gervaise Oakes, merely act in accordance with lesser principles. In all these books, however, Cooper clearly depicts the serious moral and social consequences of a disrupted society.

Not that Cooper believed that a society could be frozen in a particular state and kept unchanged indefinitely, for he clearly perceived that a principle of change was always at war with social stability. He certainly showed the stultifying effects of an unchanging social order in *The Bravo* and *The Headsman,* novels which illustrate the evil results of social organizations which make no provision at all for gradual evolution. Throughout his career he consistently opposed the principle of aristocracy, the attempt by a social class to perpetuate itself and its power. The Venetian Senate, the nobles of Berne, the lords of Leaphigh, and Major Bulstrode are all dismissed as proponents of a social stability that is bought at a price of frustration of those talented and virtuous men who are forever denied a chance to rise in society. Even in the Littlepage series, which has sometimes been misinterpreted as approving an aristocratic order, Cooper is careful to portray the evolutionary change that occurs from book to book and to make the point that the tenants, in a land-rich country like the United States, have always had the option of striking out on their own to establish their freeholds. The conflict between the need for order and the need for change is thus a constant theme in Cooper's work, and it provides the dramatic tension in some of his most successful novels.

This conflict is perhaps most clearly seen in the Leatherstocking tales, a series of novels that explores the problem in the most penetrating manner. Certainly the first three are almost entirely concerned with this theme. By invading the wilderness and seizing the lands of the Indians, the whites disrupt the red man's life, destroy the game, and wreak havoc with the natural scene. Leatherstocking, the man who has seen the proper course of conduct revealed in the harmony of nature, protests the ravishing of his beloved forests by men like Ishmael Bush or, indeed, the settlers of Templeton, who feel none of the restraints the hunter has adopted as a result of his long life in the wilderness. For these men, Judge Temple must impose the civil law; and in its meshes Leatherstocking, who does not need it, inevitably falls. The just man suffers that there shall be justice, all in the name of the Christian society which *The Pioneers,* like *The Oak Openings,* affirms as the higher good. Change is inevitable, Cooper seems to say—and especially the change that replaces the unadorned wilderness with civilized society; but in the process, he is careful to warn his readers, care must be taken that the fundamental system of values that Leatherstocking has lived by shall not be lost in the greedy exploitation of the wilderness. Upon this principle of self-restraint alone must the good and lasting democratic society be based.

That fallible man can be trusted, however, to exercise the proper self-control is an article of democratic faith that Cooper always doubted. As early as *The Pilot* he had raised the serious question of men's ability to govern themselves. He certainly perceived the inevitable results of absolute freedom among men who, abandoning the sometimes unjust civil law, decide to go it alone in the wilderness. If they do not have the moral strength of Leatherstocking, they are likely to become the lawless egoists we find portrayed in Ishmael Bush, Hurry Harry, Tom Hutter, or Aaron Thousand-acres. Even in society, moreover, men may choose to follow only the letter of the law and barely skirt the edge of criminality to achieve their ends. Such unprincipled men, like Ithuel Bolt or Jason Newcome, are, to use Cooper's expression, only "law honest." Their true motivation is purely personal greed. Finally, there is a whole class of men, like Deacon Pratt or Thomas Goldencalf, who are perhaps not fundamentally evil, but whose whole mainspring of action is desire for personal wealth. Cooper had attacked this vice in Mr. Wharton in *The Spy,* had shown the evils of a commercial oligarchy in *The Bravo,* and had warned his fellow citizens throughout his social criticism of the danger that faced the country if a commercial class supplanted the landed one at the top of the social order.

Equally dangerous, moreover, are those who assert their egoism in the political sphere. These are the ones—like Steadfast Dodge or the leveling democrats in *The Crater*—who, totally devoid of humility, see themselves as absolute equals of all other men and pervert the meaning of democracy in their belief that a majority can do no wrong. Even when they are aware of their own liability to error, they make the mistake of believing that an infallible whole can be made up of fallible parts. They are the unrestrained men of *Home as Found, The Redskins,* and *The Ways of the Hour;* men who, if not controlled by the order of constitutional government, will change the fundamental law at the whim of a manipulated majority and overturn the order of society in every generation. Cooper goes out of his way to demonstrate his belief in man's fallibility, for recognition of this fact he saw as fundamental to a well-run democracy. From *The Spy* through *The Ways of the Hour* he had treated the difficulty of seeing reality through the appearance of things. *The Bravo, Wyandotté,* the Miles Wallingford novels—all stress the inability of even well-disposed men to pierce the mask that conceals the real world and the true motives of men. How important it is then, he repeatedly argues, that men be not too certain that their opinions—the opinions of their class, or, indeed, those of a majority—are absolutely right.

Even the most intelligent of men can fall into error. Indeed, if the seeker after truth relies too strongly upon his mind alone, he will, in Cooper's view, fall into the most serious error of all—the infidelity that comes with the deification of man and his reason. This error most frequently occurs in those who give themselves over to science; for, although Cooper was himself a man of wide scientific interests, he did not believe that science alone could lead men to ultimate truth. Dr. Bat in *The Prairie* is Cooper's first caricatured picture of a scientific rationalist, a type that he presented more realistically in the atheist revolutionary Raoul Yvard in *The Wing-and-Wing.* Both he and Roswell Gardiner, the Deist in *The Sea Lions,* represent the extreme of this view. Since they will admit nothing that their senses cannot perceive nor their minds understand, they make the gross mistake of accepting as absolute truth the conclusions they reach through the use of fallible and untrustworthy instruments. In effect, they make their own erring minds the standards by which all things in the universe are to be judged. From first to last, therefore, Cooper clearly showed his fundamental distrust of unaided human reason, a distrust which grew increasingly strong as the years passed until what was food for satire in *The Prairie* became the subject for profound criticism in *The Ways of the Hour.*

How then, one might well ask, could Cooper remain a serious democrat if he distrusted so gravely the abilities of the very men upon whom the success of democratic government must ultimately rest? The answer is simple. Like many another political thinker, Cooper was a democrat, not because democracy is perfect, but only because there is no better way to order society. Aristocracy he detested as strongly as he did oligarchy—including the commercial one he saw rising in America. Democracy was the only hope; for, if properly conducted, it promised the means for uniting stability and change in one social order. He insisted, however, that democracy did not mean absolute liberty but only limited freedom under proper restraints. The problem was to insure that the restraints be applied and that they work. Throughout his career Cooper clearly saw that such restraints must come through a religious view of the world. At first he affirmed in such characters as Leatherstocking and Long Tom Coffin the proper spirit of humility that man might achieve by living among the immensity and power of untouched nature. Surely any man who lived so, Cooper seems to imply, should perceive his own insignificance in the vastness of the virgin landscape, his weakness in relation to the might of angry seas.

For this reason many of his characters such as Miles Wallingford, Mark Woolston, and Roswell Gardiner are taught the lesson of their own insignificance so that they might develop the spirit of humility they need as good members of a free society. But Cooper certainly came to realize as he grew older that such experience was not enough. Ishmael Bush and Aaron Thousandacres are unaffected by the natural scene. Another element is necessary in the process—the actual adherence to the principles of the Christian religion. To be sure, Cooper had developed an explicitly Christian theme as early as *The Wept of Wish-ton-Wish,* but this element did not become a major one in his work until *The Deerslayer.* Thereafter, in *Wyandotté, The Oak Openings,* and *The Sea Lions,* the Christian theme becomes dominant. Nor did Cooper merely affirm the abstract Christian virtues. Since man contains an immense capacity to delude himself, he distrusted the radical Protestant churches almost as much as he distrusted the leveling democrats; and he came to believe finally that the proper restraints must be found in one of the conservative Christian churches like the Episcopalian, where belief is not subject to change at the will of the congregation. Only in terms of immutable principle can democratic man find the controls he needs to assure the proper continuity and stability in a gradually evolving society.

Thus, the apparent dichotomy between Cooper's moral and social themes disappears entirely when his novels are perceived in this light. The two unite in the character of his Christian gentleman, who always represents the standard of both moral and social value in his tales. Cooper did not foresee the coming upheavals of Civil War and industrialization that were to transform American society. He clung to an agrarian ideal of a stable order ruled by the landed gentleman who, properly schooled and with leisure to study and learn, would stand at the top of the social pyramid. He would give direction and tone to society and, by the sheer weight of virtue, influence those below him in the social scale. But although he would be a gentleman in the strict meaning of the word, he would not be an aristocrat; for he would have no more political power than those with less education and wealth. Without special power, Cooper believed, such men would never be able to form the kind of oligarchy he had attacked in *The Bravo.* Cooper insisted, moreover, that education and training would teach his gentlemen heroes humility, and he always insured their restraint by making them devout members of a conservative church. To a man, they are all Episcopalians.[4]

Cooper, of course, never found the means to objectify all the elements of his broad vision of life in a single tale. The individual books emphasize one or another aspect of his world view; the critic, therefore, must view his work as a whole to understand his impressive accomplishment. Admittedly, there are flaws in his books. He was never able, for example, to draw a completely satisfactory picture of nineteenth-century American society. Venice he drew very well; contemporary New York he simply could not present. Thus, his novels of explicit social criticism are by far the weakest. The adventurous elements in *Homeward Bound* intrude upon the social theme that Cooper starts to develop; the series of incidents and vignettes presented in *Home as Found* make for a rather incoherent, unintegrated book. *The Redskins* fails too because of the amount of undramatized argument it contains. Indeed, not until *The Ways of the Hour* did Cooper finally achieve a degree of success in uniting plot and theme in a reasonably well-integrated whole. In it he at last had a subject suitable for the illustration of his distrust of the common man. As usual, however, Cooper found it difficult not to lecture his readers, and the book is far from being among his best work.

Only when Cooper turned away from the contemporary scene did he succeed in presenting a convincing social theme. Contemporary America only aroused his anger with disastrous results to his art. The Venetian republic, however, and eighteenth-century New York were far enough removed in time for him to portray the characters and settings with the balance needed in any serious art. *The Bravo* presents a convincing picture of a complex social organization drawn with the circumstantial detail that gives it life in its own right and that helps to generate its truly significant meaning. *The Pioneers* and *Satanstoe* reveal more simple societies that not only have the appearance of truth in themselves but also contribute much to the central theme. In all three tales, Cooper is content to let the interplay of character, setting, and action carry the weight of his meaning. Cooper was always more successful, too, when he drew his characters from a relatively low social class. Not that all of his gentlemen heroes are as stiff as the wooden Edward Effingham— Miles Wallingford is a notable exception—but most of them, including perhaps Judge Temple himself, suffer a bit from idealization. For this reason, *The Pathfinder* remains a better social novel than either of the "Home" volumes because it is developed in terms of more believable characters who act within the frame of a coherent social order.

Although he achieved a significant degree of success in some of his social tales, Cooper will always be best remembered for those which develop more specifically moral themes. Certainly *The Spy,* his first great success, must be considered one of his most important works if only because he developed in it the basic technique of most of his moral tales: the use of the physical setting to define the fundamental issue in the novel. The neutral ground becomes in itself an essential factor in the action, for the meaning of the tale derives in large part from the relation of the various characters to that environment. This interplay of character and setting always remained an effective device in Cooper and one that he learned to use in a variety of ways. In *The Spy,* he uses it to illustrate the disparity between appearance and reality in the external world; and this theme he was to develop again with great success in *Wyandotté,* in which Captain Willoughby consistently fails to see the true nature of reality; and in the Miles Wallingford novels in which the relation of Miles to his environment, both afloat and ashore, finally reveals to him the deceptiveness of external reality and leads to the final affirmation of more permanent values than those of the workaday world.

The technique, of course, yielded its best results in the Leatherstocking tales in which the moral value of the landscape is most artistically developed. Least important perhaps in *The Pathfinder,* the physical setting is of the utmost significance in the other four tales. The darkness and the density of the virgin forest that stretches unbroken from the Hudson to the Mississippi are all but tactilely felt in *The Last of the Mohicans* and *The Deerslayer.* The outposts of civilization are practically swallowed up in the dense wilderness that surrounds them, a fact of great importance in interpreting the meaning of the action. In *The Prairie,* too, the immensity of the hostile landscape, which dwarfs the characters who move through it, contributes to our understanding of the meaning involved in the characters of the trapper, Dr. Bat and Ishmael Bush. Only in *The Pioneers* does man meet nature on something like equal terms; but the illusion of dominance that some of the characters acquire leads to wanton, immoral waste of the resources they possess. In the light of this environment, Leatherstocking's forbearance and the settlers' selfishness take qn a moral meaning that has far-reaching ramifications both in the society that Judge Temple is trying to organize and in American civilization as a whole. The repetition of this theme in *The Chainbearer* through similar use of character and setting further reveals the importance of this device in Cooper's moral fiction.

Other elements in nature besides the American wilderness function, of course, in this way throughout Cooper's work. His use of ships at sea in *The Pilot* and *Homeward Bound* to illustrate the need for educated and virtuous authority, both in the Pilot himself and in Captain Truck, is obvious enough. Equally significant, however, is Cooper's use of marine storms to measure heroes like Miles Wallingford and Roswell Gardiner against the forces of nature in order to teach them their fallibility and weakness before the power of Him who rules the cosmos. The most extreme use that Cooper makes of this device comes late with the earthquakes in *The Crater* and with the antarctic winter in *The Sea Lions*. These may be criticized, perhaps, as much too manipulated to have the ring of truth. On the other hand, their use also reveals Cooper's apparent belief that the function of his early and more common descriptions of nature in the tales of wilderness and sea had not been understood by his audience. Leatherstocking's reaction to the suggestive value of the virgin forest or to the immense barrenness of the Great Plains is no different from Mark Woolston's reactions to the earthquakes or Gardiner's to the antarctic winter. That Cooper makes the natural phenomena increasingly violent bespeaks the importance he attached both to the theme and to the means of expression. He was obviously trying to make sure that his meaning would be understood.

Finally, we may observe the artistic devices Cooper used to express his explicitly Christian themes. The natural landscape certainly provided a means for presenting a broadly religious view, but it would not do as well for expressing specifically Christian concepts. In *The Wept of Wish-ton-Wish* and *The Deerslayer*, however, Cooper found the means he needed: through the use of characters in action—the Heathcotes and Hetty Hutter—he affirmed the fundamental Christian virtues that form the ideal in those books. Through the behavior of contrasting characters, like the Reverend Meek

Wolfe, Tom Hutter, and Hurry Harry, he was able to illustrate how far below that ideal the mass of men fall. In *The Oak Openings,* moreover, the actions of men in the American wilderness are made to suggest the Crucifixion in the death of Parson Amen and its far-reaching effects in the conversion of Scalping Peter, a truly remarkable artistic achievement in an otherwise imperfect novel. Cooper is alone among nineteenth-century American writers in using the truths of Christianity as the subject for serious art;[5] and, by and large, he is quite successful in giving them objective expression in works that are also convincing in terms of plot, character, and setting.

The moral emphasis everywhere apparent in Cooper's work and the religious expression that he sometimes chose to give it have probably been, as Brady believes (p. 96), major reasons for the decline of Cooper's popularity in the twentieth century. He writes from a largely unpopular point of view, and he openly criticizes some tenets that modern society holds dear. To say this, however, is not to imply a limitation on Cooper's part, but one of his audience. Surely we owe him the objectivity to see his work for what it is and does and to read it in his terms rather than ours if we wish to estimate justly his artistic accomplishment. We can certainly agree that he looked to the heart of American society and was basically sound in his analysis of democracy. We need only look at our own society to agree with him that democracy tends to mediocrity—a high average of accomplishment with little true excellence. We are perhaps equally concerned in the twentieth century as he was in the nineteenth with the pressures of group conformity, and we can understand the discomfort of Aristabulus Bragg who feared his neighbors' opinions. We are certainly as aware as Cooper was of the weakness of human reason and the fallibility of democratic opinion. For these reasons and many others, the twentieth-century reader can return with interest and profit to Cooper, the moralist and social critic.

That we can return with pleasure to Cooper the artist is equally true. To be sure, he sometimes wrote weak novels; and we would not recommend *Lionel Lincoln, Mercedes of Castile,* or *The Redskins* to the general reader. But many other books are worthy of close attention and study. Once we learn to accept the old-fashioned and sometimes careless style, we can come to appreciate Cooper's fundamental artistry. His use of the natural landscape, his fine sense of the physical environment, and the meanings he can generate from the actions of his characters in plot and setting - more than make up for the relatively minor deficiencies of his major works. The man who could write *The Spy, The Pilot,* the five Leatherstocking tales, *The Wept of Wish-ton-Wish, The Bravo,* the five moral tales of the early 1840's, and the first two Littlepage novels—as well as certain excellent parts of less successful works—is clearly a serious artist whose range of expression is rather wide and whose themes are still of interest to thoughtful men of the twentieth century. If he failed in his social novels, he succeeded brilliantly in some of his moral ones. If he shared the limitations of his time and background, he was sometimes able to rise above the restrictions that his age and society placed upon him. If his career is marked by frequent failure, he also accomplished much in his thirty years as a novelist. To see his work for what it is and to understand its means of expression is, therefore, to recognize James Fenimore Cooper as a major American artist.

Notes and References

Quotations from Cooper's novels are from the Darley-Townsend edition, New York, 1859-1861. Page references in the text are to the individual volumes, identified by title, in this edition. The full reference to secondary sources is given only once below. Thereafter, whenever a biographer or critic is named in the text, a page reference following the quoted material indicates that his work has already been cited. Page references to Robert E. Spiller's work in the text are to his *Fenimore Cooper: Critic of His Times;* other works by Spiller are specified by title.

Chapter One

1. For a full discussion of Cooper's entry into authorship and the possible identification of his source, see George E. Hastings, "How Cooper Became a Novelist," *American Literature,* XII (1940), 20-51.

2. Marius Bewley, *The Eccentric Design* (New York, 1959), p. 47.

3. "Fenimore Cooper's Literary Offenses," *The Writings of Mark Twain* (New York, 1911), XXII, 78-96.

4. R. W. B. Lewis, "Hold on Hard to the Huckleberry Bushes," *Sewanee Review,* LXVII (1959), 468. Brady's fine essay is "Myth-Maker and Christian Romancer," *American Classics Reconsidered: A Christian Appraisal,* ed. Harold C. Gardiner, S.J. (New York, 1958), pp. 59-97.

5. The three most useful biographies are Thomas R. Lounsbury, *James Fenimore Cooper* (Boston, 1883); Robert E. Spiller, *Fenimore Cooper: Critic of His Times* (New York, 1931); James Grossman, *James Fenimore Cooper* (New York, 1949). That by Henry W. Boynton, *James Fenimore Cooper* (New York, 1931), contains almost no criticism; that by Marcel Clavel, *Fenimore Cooper, Sa Vie et Son Oeuvre: La Jeunesse* (Aix-en-Provence, 1938), covers only the years to 1826. A critical biography is in preparation by James Franklin Beard, the editor of Cooper's *Letters and Journals.*

6. "Prose and Pictures: James Fenimore Cooper," *Tulane Studies in English,* III (1952), 136-37.

7. An able defense of Cooper's female characters is W. C. Brownell, *American Prose Masters* (New York, 1923), pp. 34-41.

See also Lucy L. Hazard, *The Frontier in American Literature* (New York, 1927), pp. 100-3.

8. Yvor Winters, *Maule's Curse* (Norfolk, Conn., 1938), pp. 25-50.

9. *Notes on Life and Letters* (London, 1925), p. 55. See also Edward E. Hale, Jr., "American Scenery in Cooper's Novels," *Sewanee Review*, XVIII (1910), 317-32, which stresses Cooper's realism and the suggestion of spaciousness in his forest descriptions. A more recent discussion of the spatial element in Cooper is R. W. B. Lewis, *The American Adam* (Chicago, 1955), pp. 98-105.

10. For a good brief discussion of Cooper's moral vision of life and its relation to that of his contemporaries, see the article by Howard Mumford Jones cited in note 6 above, esp. pp. 143-47.

Chapter Two

1. *The Letters and Journals of James Fenimore Cooper*, ed. by James Franklin Beard (Cambridge, Mass., 1960), I, 49.

2. The facts of publication explain the abrupt ending of *The Spy*. As Cooper wrote in the 1849 preface (included in the Darley-Townsend edition), the last chapter was actually printed and paged before the previous ones were written, so that the novel would not develop to extreme length; hence, "the manner in which the actors are hurried off the scene" (p. xi).

3. The pertinent passages from this preface are most easily found in Arvid Shulenberger, *Cooper's Theory of Fiction* (Lawrence, Kansas, 1955), pp. 16-17. See also *Letters and Journals*, I, 44, wherein Cooper complains that it is difficult to make native materials interesting to American readers.

4. *Notions of the Americans: Picked Up by a Travelling Bachelor* (London, 1828), II, 142-43.

5. Although Bewley seems to have perceived the imaginative importance of this setting, he simply mentions it without pursuing its implications for the novel as a whole (p. 77).

6. For a discussion of Cooper's stylistic revisions in this novel, see Tremaine McDowell, "James Fenimore Cooper as Self-Critic," *Studies in Philology*, XXVII (1930), 508-16.

7. Also published in 1823 was *Tales' for Fifteen*, a pair of stories in the style of Mrs. Opie that Cooper had probably written early in 1821 during the time he had given up work on *The Spy* and that his publisher later pressed him for. See James Franklin Beard, ed., *Tales for Fifteen* by James Fenimore Cooper (Gainesville, Fla.: Scholars' Facsimiles and Reprints, 1959), Introduction.

8. Indeed, the judge has seen this weakness in himself when he too was carried away in the destruction of the pigeons and later regretted his actions (pp. 273-74).

9. See especially Grossman, pp. 40-41.

10. For contemporary British comment about this strange implication, see Marcel Clavel, *Fenimore Cooper and His Critics* (Aix-en-Provence, 1938), pp. 275-76.

11. Winters, pp. 44-45; Grossman, p. 41; Bewley, pp. 74, 319.

12. Typical views are expressed in Robert H. Zoellner, "Conceptual Ambivalence in Cooper's Leatherstocking," *American Literature*, XXXI (1960), 407; and in Grossman, p. 43.

13. Henry Nash Smith, ed., *The Prairie* by James Fenimore Cooper, Rinehart ed. (New York, 1949), xiv-xv. See also Smith's *Virgin Land* (New York, 1957), pp. 256-60.

14. For a full discussion of the attitudes toward nature expressed in *The Prairie*, see my article, "Man and Nature in Cooper's *The Prairie*," *Nineteenth-Century Fiction*, XV (1961), pp. 313-23.

15. James T. Flanagan, "The Authenticity of Cooper's *The Prairie*," *Modern Language Quarterly*, II (1941), 99-104.

16. Grossman, p. 48.

17. See especially Harry Hayden Clark, "Fenimore Cooper and Science," *Transactions of the Wisconsin Academy of Sciences, Arts, and Letters*, XLVIII (1959), 179-204; XLIX (1960), 249-82.

18. I am leaving out of account here his *Notions of the Americans* (1828) largely because a detailed consideration of Cooper's non-fiction is beyond the scope of this study. It will be touched upon as needed, however, in the discussion of the novels. See Chapter Three.

19. Cooper might well have reversed this judgment, for his letters seem to indicate that he thought rather less of *The Wept of Wish-ton-Wish* than of *The Red Rover* or *The Water-Witch*. See *Letters and Journals*, I, 258, 396. Cooper, however, was never an accurate judge of his own work, and his stated opinions must always be heavily discounted.

20. The character of Ruth explains the somewhat puzzling title. She is the one mourned for, the "Wept" of the valley. Cooper explains the Wish-ton-Wish as the whippoorwill. Albert Keiser, however, in *The Indian in American Literature* (New York, 1933), p. 109, defines the word as "prairie dog."

21. Grossman criticizes Cooper for not making more of this material (p. 70). It seems to me, however, that Cooper is rather to be commended not only for including the theme of miscege-

nation in a book written in the early nineteenth century but for making the Heathcotes consistent in accepting the child as good Christians should. Cf. the interesting, if rather extreme, discussion of Cooper's use of miscegenation in Leslie A. Fiedler, *Love and Death in the American Novel* (New York, 1960), pp. 200-6.

Chapter Three

1. *Letters and Journals,* I, 411.
2. For a discussion of Cooper's part in the Polish question, see Robert E. Spiller, "Fenimore Cooper and Lafayette: Friends of Polish Freedom, 1830-1832," *American Literature,* VII (1935), 56-75.
3. Although discussion of the finance controversy, a French domestic issue, into which Cooper was drawn out of friendship with Lafayette, is beyond the scope of this study, the controversy is important in that adverse reactions in America to Cooper's part in it influenced to some extent his later decision to retire as a novelist. For a full discussion of the controversy, see Robert E. Spiller, "Fenimore Cooper and Lafayette: The Finance Controversy of 1831-1832," *American Literature,* III (1931), 28-44.
4. *Letters and Journals,* II, 80.
5. *Ibid.,* II, 4, 75, 77-78, *passim.*
6. Bewley, pp. 58-60. Cf. Russell Kirk, "Cooper and the European Puzzle," *College English,* VII (1946), 199.
7. Bewley, p. 49. For other opinions, see Spiller, p. 220; Beard, *Letters and Journals,* II, 121.
8. *Letters and Journals,* II, 175, 368.
9. For a full discussion of the attacks on Cooper in the Whig press, see Dorothy Waples, *The Whig Myth of James Fenimore Cooper* (New Haven, Conn., 1938).
10. Also published in 1838 was *The Chronicles of Cooperstown,* a pedestrian factual account of local history.
11. Thus, in *Home as Found,* Steadfast Dodge announces: "To my notion, gentlemen and ladies, God never intended an American to kneel" (p. 219)!
12. Before the appearance of these novels, however, Cooper had published in 1839 *The History of the ˙Navy of the United States of America,* the first full history of the Navy and still a useful one.
13. Cooper was planning a tale of the forest and Lake Ontario while he was still in Europe early in 1831. See *Letters and Journals,* II, 53.

14. Grossman notes the mixed reception of both *The Pathfinder* and *The Deerslayer*, pp. 151-52.

15. Brady, p. 94. See also D. H. Lawrence, *Studies in Classic American Literature* (New York, 1953), p. 72.

16. Cf. Bewley's excellent analysis of the character of Hurry Harry and his relation to Deerslayer, pp. 95-96.

Chapter Four

1. This darkening of Cooper's view of the world is the only effect one can see of the specific difficulties that Cooper faced in the early 1840's. One looks in vain in his novels for any important influence of the long series of libel suits in which he was engaged while writing such tales as *The Two Admirals, The Wing-and-Wing,* and *Wyandotté.*

2. Although Cooper's reputation fell, perhaps because of a conspiracy of silence among the newspapers (Grossman, p. 188), the sales of his books actually were higher than they had been in the 1820's. *The Wing-and-Wing* and *Wyandotté* sold twice as well as *The Spy* and *The Pioneers,* though the returns to the author were small because of the "economic and book trade crisis of the early forties." See William Charvat, "Cooper as Professional Author," *James Fenimore Cooper: A Re-Appraisal* (Cooperstown, N. Y., 1954), pp. 128-43.

3. Of the biographers and critics, only Grossman has discussed these novels at length; the others give them as a rule only cursory notice. None of them treat the moral and religious themes with the seriousness that Cooper clearly intended, nor do they attempt to relate the novels to one another in any way.

4. Grossman also comments upon the solid reality of the details and the philosophical questions raised by the action—questions that Cooper personally remains aloof from answering (pp. 157-58). Grossman does not see the issue, however, as fundamentally one of moral choice.

5. Cf. Grossman, p. 234.

6. Cf. Grossman's analysis of the characters of the English officers and of Ithuel Bolt, which covers many of these points (pp. 163-65).

7. Also published in 1843 was *Autobiography of a Pocket Handkerchief,* a slight magazine piece that afterwards appeared in book form but was never included in his collected works. The book contains a rather biting attack upon commercial society, which assigns a pecuniary value to everything; it includes a good

deal of satire on New York society reminiscent of *Home as Found;* and it affirms the alternative value of moral and religious truth.

8. I have not considered the question of Cooper's "idealization" of the Indians, mainly because the issue is by no means central to the interpretation of the novels. Moreover, the evidence indicates that Cooper followed the best sources available to him in his depiction of the Indians. See Brownell, pp. 16-20; Keiser, pp. 101-43; Gregory Paine, "The Indians of the Leather-Stocking Tales," *Studies in Philology,* XXIII (1926), 16-39; J. A. Russell, "Cooper: Interpreter of the Real and Historical Indian," *Journal of American History,* XXIII (1929), 41-71; John T. Frederick, "Cooper's Eloquent Indians," *PMLA,* LXXI (1956), 1004-17.

9. Cf. Grossman, p. 175, and Bewley, pp. 79-81, both of whom treat *Wyandotté* in relation to *The Spy* and *Lionel Lincoln.*

10. Following *Wyandotté* in 1843, Cooper also published *Ned Myers,* the narrative of the life of an old shipmate on board the *Stirling,* who had recently written to and visited Cooper. The tale itself is much more racy in style than Cooper's usual work and probably represents, as Cooper claimed, an edited version of Ned's own account.

11. It is true, of course, as every critic has observed, that to some extent Miles resembles Cooper himself in his career and his opinions, that Lucy Hardinge may represent in some degree Cooper's picture of his own wife (Lounsbury, pp. 249-51). Such details, however, do not justify our reading the novel as biography. Rather, too much stress on them may get in the way of our seeing the novel for what it is—a serious work of fiction.

Chapter Five

1. Good brief discussions of the anti-rent struggle can be found in Spiller, pp. 306-13, and Grossman, pp. 197-219. See also Granville Hicks, "Landlord Cooper and the Anti-Renters," *Antioch Review,* V (1945), 95-109. A highly readable history of the struggle by Henry Christman, *Tin Horns and Calico* (New York, 1945), is strongly slanted in favor of the tenants.

2. See especially David M. Ellis, "The Coopers and New York State Landholding Systems," *James Fenimore Cooper: A Re-Appraisal* (Cooperstown, N. Y., 1954), p. 50.

3. For a discussion of the Littlepage series as an artistic unit, see my article, "Cooper's Littlepage Novels: Change and Stability in American Society," *American Literature,* XXXII (1960), 280-90.

4. For a brief discussion of the social groups to be found in *Satanstoe,* see Richard Chase, *The American Novel and Its Tradition* (New York, 1957), pp. 48-49.

5. Cf. Grossman, p. 209.

6. In 1846, Cooper also published *Lives of Distinguished American Naval Officers,* a collection of short biographies that had appeared in *Graham's Magazine* between 1842 and 1845.

7. To distinguish the disguised tenants from the real red men he later introduces in the tale, Cooper calls the false Indians "Injins" throughout.

8. Cf. Brady, p. 80, on the function of the Negro and Indian in the novel.

9. For a full discussion of the moral theme in *The Crater,* see my article "Cooper's *The Crater* and the Moral Basis of Society," *Papers of the Michigan Academy of Science, Arts, and Letters,* XLIV (1959), 371-80. Other views may be found in Harold H. Scudder, "Cooper's *The Crater,*" *American Literature,* XIX (1947), 109-26; John C. McCloskey, "Cooper's Political Views in *The Crater,*" *Modern Philology,* LIII (1955), 113-16; George J. Becker, "James Fenimore Cooper and American Democracy," *College English,* XVII (1956), 332.

10. Cf. Grossman, p. 222.

11. W. B. Gates, "A Note on Cooper and *Robinson Crusoe,*" *Modern Language Notes,* LXVII (1952), 421-22.

12. *The Crater,* pp. 113, 175-76, in which Mark sees his islands as a "new world" or "new creation," and pp. 198, 223-24, in which he sees himself and Bridget as a new Adam and Eve in the Garden of Eden.

13. Lounsbury, p. 255; Grossman, pp. 225-26.

14. Howard Mumford Jones, *The Pursuit of Happiness* (Cambridge, Mass., 1953), p. 111.

15. Brady, p. 81; Grossman, p. 230.

16. Brady, p. 81; Bewley, p. 189. A better analysis, similar in some respects to what follows here, is Grossman, pp. 231-35.

17. A more detailed discussion of this book is in my article, "Cooper's Last Novels, 1847-1850," *PMLA,* LXXV (1960), 583-90.

Chapter Six

1. Cooper's play had three performances, June 18-20, 1850; it has never been published. We can get some idea of its quality, however, from a plot summary in a contemporary newspaper and from a single scene that was published by William E. Burton,

Cyclopaedia of Wit and Humor (New York, 1858), pp. 297-99. See John A. Kouwenhoven, "Cooper's 'Upside Down' Turns Up," *Colophon,* III n. s. (1938), 524-30.

2. These are "The Lake Gun," a short piece written for a miscellany, *The Parthenon* (1850) and an essay "American and European Scenery Compared," published in *The Home Book of the Picturesque* (New York, 1852), pp. 51-69. *The Lake Gun* was reprinted (New York, 1932) with an introduction by Robert E. Spiller.

3. An incomplete text of the Introduction to this book, reprinted from a newspaper, *The Spirit of the Fair* (1864), is to be found in Dixon Ryan Fox, ed., *New York,* by James Fenimore Cooper (New York, 1930). This is supplemented by James Franklin Beard, "The First History of Greater New York: Unknown Portions of Fenimore Cooper's Last Work," *The New-York Historical Society Quarterly,* XXXVII (1953), 109-45. Beard includes the unpublished parts of the Introduction and the fragments of text that have survived in page proof.

4. To be sure, Judge Temple in *The Pioneers* has a Quaker background, but Cooper specifically states that even he had become an Episcopalian, at least in form, by the time of the action of the novel (p. 110).

5. Brady, pp. 81, 96.

Selected Bibliography

PRIMARY SOURCES

This bibliography is selective. It contains all of Cooper's major fiction, but only that non-fiction which is likely to be of use to the general student in understanding Cooper's thought or interpreting his art. For a complete bibliography of Cooper's works, see Robert E. Spiller and Philip C. Blackburn, *A Descriptive Bibliography of the Writings of James Fenimore Cooper* (New York, 1934), upon which the following material is based. Titles, publishers, and dates are those of the first American editions. Beginning with *The Prairie*, however, the British edition usually preceded the American, sometimes by as much as several months. The British title or date is given whenever either differs significantly from the American.

Precaution: A Novel. New York: A. T. Goodrich & Co., 1820.

The Spy: A Tale of the Neutral Ground. New York: Wiley and Halstead, 1821.

The Pioneers; or, The Sources of the Susquehanna: A Descriptive Tale. New York: Charles Wiley, 1823.

Tales for Fifteen; or, Imagination and Heart. New York: Charles Wiley, 1823.

The Pilot: A Tale of the Sea. New York: Charles Wiley, 1824.

Lionel Lincoln; or, The Leaguer of Boston. New York: Charles Wiley, 1825.

The Last of the Mohicans: A Narrative of 1757. Philadelphia: Carey and Lea, 1826.

The Prairie: A Tale. Philadelphia: Carey, Lea, and Carey, 1827.

The Red Rover: A Tale. Philadelphia: Carey, Lea, and Carey, 1828.

(The first British edition had already appeared late in 1827.)

Notions of the Americans: Picked Up by a Travelling Bachelor. Philadelphia: Carey, Lea, and Carey, 1828.

The Wept of Wish-ton-Wish: A Tale. Philadelphia: Carey, Lea, and Carey, 1829. British title: *The Borderers: A Tale.*

The Water-Witch; or, The Skimmer of the Seas: A Tale. Philadelphia: Carey and Lea, 1830.

The Bravo: A Tale. Philadelphia: Carey and Lea, 1831.

The Heidenmauer; or, The Benedictines: A Legend of the Rhine. Philadelphia: Carey and Lea, 1832.

The Headsman; or, The Abbaye des Vignerons: A Tale. Philadelphia: Carey, Lea, and Blanchard, 1833.

A Letter to His Countrymen. New York: John Wiley, 1834.

The Monikins. Philadelphia: Carey, Lea, and Blanchard, 1835.

Sketches of Switzerland. Philadelphia: Carey, Lea, and Blanchard, 1836. British title: *Excursions in Switzerland.*

Sketches of Switzerland: Part Second. Philadelphia: Carey, Lea, and Blanchard, 1836. British title: *A Residence in France; with an Excursion up the Rhine, and a Second Visit to Switzerland.*

Gleanings in Europe: [France]. Philadelphia: Carey, Lea, and Blanchard, 1837. British title: *Recollections of Europe.*

Gleanings in Europe: England. Philadelphia: Carey, Lea, and Blanchard, 1837. British title: *England, with Sketches of Society in the Metropolis.*

Gleanings in Europe: Italy. Philadelphia: Carey, Lea, and Blanchard, 1838. British title: *Excursions in Italy.*

The American Democrat; or, Hints on the Social and Civic Relations of the United States of America. Cooperstown, N. Y.: H. & E. Phinney, 1838.

The Chronicles of Cooperstown. Cooperstown, N. Y.: H. & E. Phinney, 1838.

Homeward Bound; or, The Chase: A Tale of the Sea. Philadelphia: Carey, Lea, and Blanchard, 1838.

Home as Found. Philadelphia: Lea and Blanchard, 1838. British title: *Eve Effingham; or, Home.*

The History of the Navy of the United States of America. Philadelphia: Lee and Blanchard, 1839.

The Pathfinder; or, The Inland Sea. Philadelphia: Lea and Blanchard, 1840.

Mercedes of Castile; or, The Voyage to Cathay. Philadelphia: Lea and Blanchard, 1840.

The Deerslayer; or, The First War-Path: A Tale. Philadelphia: Lea and Blanchard, 1841.

The Two Admirals: A Tale. Philadelphia: Lea and Blanchard, 1842.

The Wing-and-Wing; or, Le Feu-Follet: A Tale. Philadelphia: Lea and Blanchard, 1842. British title: *The Jack O'Lantern (Le Feu Follet); or, The Privateer.*

Le Mouchoir: An Autobiographical Romance. New York: Wilson & Co., Brother Jonathan Press, 1843. Has also appeared as

Autobiography of a Pocket Handkerchief. British title: *The French Governess; or, The Embroidered Handkerchief.*

Wyandotté; or, The Hutted Knoll: A Tale. Philadelphia: Lea and Blanchard, 1843.

Ned Myers; or, A Life Before the Mast. Philadelphia: Lea and Blanchard, 1843.

Afloat and Ashore; or, The Adventures of Miles Wallingford (two series). Philadelphia: Published by the Author, 1844. Subsequent American editions retitle the second part *Miles Wallingford.* First British edition retitled the second part *Lucy Hardinge*: A Second Series of Afloat and Ashore.

Satanstoe; or, The Littlepage Manuscripts: A Tale of the Colony. New York: Burgess, Stringer & Co., 1845.

The Chainbearer; or, The Littlepage Manuscripts. New York: Burgess, Stringer & Co., 1845.

Lives of Distinguished American Naval Officers. Philadelphia: Carey and Hart, 1846.

The Redskins; or, Indian and Injin: Being the Conclusion of the *Ltitlepage Manuscripts.* New York: Burgess and Stringer, 1846. British title: *Ravensnest; or, The Redskins.*

The Crater; or, Vulcan's Peak: A Tale of the Pacific. New York: Burgess, Stringer & Co., 1847. British title: *Mark's Reef; or, The Crater*: A Tale of the Pacific.

Jack Tier; or, The Florida Reef. New York: Burgess, Stringer & Co., 1848. Had appeared in *Graham's Magazine* (November 1846-March 1848) as "The Islets of the Gulf; or, Rose Budd." British title: *Captain Spike; or, The Islets of the Gulf.*

The Oak Openings; or, The Bee-Hunter. New York: Burgess, Stringer & Co., 1848. British title: *The Bee-Hunter; or, The Oak Openings.*

The Sea Lions; or, The Lost Sealers. New York: Stringer and Townsend, 1849.

The Ways of the Hour: A Tale. New York: George P. Putnam, 1850.

SECONDARY SOURCES

The following highly selective bibliography stresses the critical and evaluative studies of Cooper in preference to the biographical and historical. It includes the most important biographies and collections of letters, the best general discussions of Cooper's achievement, and those special studies that are likely to be most useful to the general student. Other books and articles are cited in the footnotes.

More complete bibliographies are in Robert E. Spiller, *James*

Fenimore Cooper: Representative Selections (New York, 1936), pp. lxxxix-cii; Spiller, Thorpe, *et al.*, *A Literary History of the United States* (New York, 1948), vol. III and Supplement. Current items may be found in the annual bibliography in *PMLA* and in each issue of *American Literature*.

BEARD, JAMES FRANKLIN. "Cooper and His Artistic Contemporaries," *James Fenimore Cooper: A Re-Appraisal* (Cooperstown, N. Y., 1954), pp. 112-27. Discusses Cooper's association with the graphic artists and the descriptive technique they shared: the expression of ideal truth through harmonization of precise details.

————, ed. *The Letters and Journals of James Fenimore Cooper* (2 vols., Cambridge, Mass., 1960). The initial volumes of the first complete edition of Cooper's letters and journals, expertly edited and thoroughly annotated; other volumes to follow.

BECKER, GEORGE J. "James Fenimore Cooper and American Democracy," *College English*, XVII (1956), 325-34. Sees Cooper as overly legalistic in his criticism of American democracy and implies, somewhat unjustly, that Cooper sought an unchanging society.

BEWLEY, MARIUS. *The Eccentric Design* (New York, 1959), pp. 47-100. Full analyses of *The Heidenmauer* and *The Bravo;* an excellent analysis of *The Deerslayer* as illustrating Cooper's skill in making physical action suggest a developing moral theme.

BRADY, CHARLES A. "Myth-Maker and Christian Romancer," *American Classics Reconsidered: A Christian Appraisal*, ed. Harold C. Gardiner, S.J. (New York, 1958), pp. 59-97. Evaluates Cooper from the Catholic point of view and discusses the mythic and epic qualities in the Leatherstocking tales.

BROWNELL, WILLIAM C. *American Prose Masters* (New York, 1923), pp. 1-50. Though first published in 1906, remains one of the best brief evaluations of Cooper's art; thoroughly sound in approach and conclusions.

CANBY, HENRY S. *Classic Americans* (New York, 1931), pp. 97-142. An interesting general study that places perhaps too much stress upon Cooper's Quaker heritage and insists too strongly upon his enthusiastic amateurism in art.

CHASE, RICHARD. *The American Novel and Its Tradition* (New York, 1957), pp. 43-65. Examines *Satanstoe* and *The Prairie* as exemplifying the conflict between "the values of traditional society and those of the lone individual in the marginal hinterland."

CLARK, HARRY H. "Fenimore Cooper and Science," *Transactions of the Wisconsin Academy of Sciences, Arts, and Letters,* XLVIII (1959), 179-204; XLIX (1960), 249-82. A thorough discussion of Cooper's generally favorable attitude toward science when properly allied with religious belief.

CLAVEL, MARCEL. *Fenimore Cooper, Sa Vie et Son Oeuvre: La Jeunesse* (Aix-en-Provence, 1938). A detailed life of Cooper to 1826 and a thorough criticism of the works through *The Last of the Mohicans* in terms of such elements as character and style.

DAVIS, DAVID BRION. "The Deerslayer, a Democratic Knight of the Wilderness," *Twelve Original Essays on Great American Novels* (Detroit, 1958), pp. 1-22. Sees Deerslayer as a combination "Homeric hero and Christian saint" whose violence is sanctified by his asceticism and his union with nature.

GROSSMAN, JAMES. "Cooper and the Responsibility of the Press," *James Fenimore Cooper: A Re-Appraisal* (Cooperstown, N. Y., 1954), pp. 144-53. Discusses the principles involved on both sides in Cooper's war with the press, with special reference to the character of Steadfast Dodge in the "Home" novels.

————. *James Fenimore Cooper* (New York, 1949). An interesting and sound biography, warmly sympathetic with its subject; especially valuable for its discriminating criticism of the novels.

JONES, HOWARD MUMFORD. "Prose and Pictures: James Fenimore Cooper," *Tulane Studies in English,* III (1952), 133-54; an important study describing the "great religious vision of life" that Cooper shared with the Hudson River painters.

————. *The Frontier in American Fiction* (Jerusalem, 1956), pp. 26-50. Discusses several of the important philosophic concepts that inform Cooper's frontier novels, especially the Leatherstocking tales.

LAWRENCE, D. H. *Studies in Classic American Literature* (New York, 1953), pp. 43-73. Not wholly accurate in fact or interpretation and highly individual in approach, but at times brilliantly perceptive (first published in 1923).

LOUNSBURY, THOMAS R. *James Fenimore Cooper* (Boston, 1883). The first of the major biographies and somewhat unsympathetic with its subject, but highly readable and still useful, though rather weak in criticism, especially of the later novels.

PARRINGTON, VERNON L. *Main Currents in American Thought* (New York, 1927-1930), II, 222-37. An important analysis of Cooper's social and political thought, but lays perhaps too much stress on the apparent dichotomy between realism and romance in Cooper's fiction.

PEARCE, ROY HARVEY. "The Leatherstocking Tales Re-Examined," *South Atlantic Quarterly*, XLVI (1947), 524-36. Concludes that the tales are essentially an artistic failure because Cooper could not objectify the forces of civilization as well as he could those of the frontier.

RINGE, DONALD A. "Cooper's Last Novels, 1847-1850," *PMLA*, LXXV (1960), 583-90. Sees the last five novels in terms of Cooper's epistemology: the balance of reason and faith as the guide to truth.

————. "Cooper's Littlepage Novels: Change and Stability in American Society," *American Literature*, XXXII (1960), 280-90. Analyzes the series as an artistic unit deriving form and meaning from the conflict between the principles of ordered and chaotic change represented by the Littlepage and Newcome families.

————. "Cooper's *The Crater* and the Moral Basis of Society," *Papers of the Michigan Academy of Science, Arts, and Letters,* XLIV (1959), 371-80. Shows the thematic relation between the early episodes in the novel and the rise and fall of the Utopian society.

————. "James Fenimore Cooper and Thomas Cole: An Analogous Technique," *American Literature*, XXX (1958), 26-36. Following Jones and Beard (q.v.), shows the use that novelist and painter made of the technique of contrasted landscapes to express similar moral themes.

————. "Man and Nature in Cooper's *The Prairie*," *Nineteenth-Century Fiction*, XV (1961), 313-23. Sees the conflict of the exploitive, moral, and scientific views of nature as fundamental to the meaning of the book.

SMITH, HENRY NASH. *Virgin Land* (New York, 1957), pp. 64-76, 246-60. Two important discussions of the Leatherstocking tales in relation to the problem of social order and the contemporary theory of the "stages of society," ranging from barbarism to civilization (first published in 1950).

SPILLER, ROBERT E. *Fenimore Cooper: Critic of His Times* (New York, 1931). An important biography stressing Cooper's social criticism; much information on his life and milieu, but relatively little criticism of his work.

————. *James Fenimore Cooper: Representative Selections* (New York, 1936). Contains a good introduction to Cooper, the social critic, supplementing the earlier biography, and a judicious sampling of Cooper's non-fiction.

————. "Second Thoughts on Cooper as a Social Critic," *James Fenimore Cooper: A Re-Appraisal* (Cooperstown, N. Y., 1954), pp. 172-89. A valuable survey of Cooper scholarship, with some important suggestions of possible methods for the future study of Cooper.

WINTERS, YVOR. *Maule's Curse* (Norfolk, Conn., 1938), pp. 25-50. One of the best short treatments of Cooper as a literary artist, with some excellent discussion of style.

ZOELLNER, ROBERT H. "Conceptual Ambivalence in Cooper's Leatherstocking," *American Literature*, XXXI (1960), 397-420. Sees the tales as aesthetically inconsistent because the "socially oriented" Cooper was unable fully to disentangle the mythic idealization of Leatherstocking from "its constraining social pattern."

Index

Characters in the novels are not included here unless referred to in discussions other than those of the specific novels in which they appear.

Afloat and Ashore, 13, 18, 20, 54-55, 91, 94, 105-9, 114, 149, 153
Amen, Parson, 135-36, 144, 155
"American and European Scenery Compared," 164
American Democrat, The, 12, 72-73, 89
American Polish Committee, 12, 57
Anti-rent war, 13, 115-17, 120, 124-25, 144
Associationist psychology, 26-28
Austen, Jane, 23
Autobiography of a Pocket Handkerchief (Le Mouchoir), 161-62

Bat, Dr. Obed, 45, 47-48, 52, 98, 137-38, 149, 153
Bewley, Marius, 18, 22, 60-62
Birch, Harvey, 28, 30-32, 40, 61, 92-93, 97, 105, 112, 133
Bluewater, Admiral Richard, 92-97, 109, 146
Bolt, Ithuel, 99-100, 113, 120, 148
Bonifacius, Abbot of Limburg, 62-63, 87
Brady, Charles A., 18, 22, 32, 49, 86-87, 127, 145, 155
Bragg, Aristabulus, 78, 155
Bravo, The, 12, 18, 58-62, 64, 66-67, 89-90, 117, 147-49, 151-52, 156
Budd, Mrs., 132-34, 136, 139
Bulstrode, Major, 118, 121, 147
Bumppo, Natty (also called Leath-erstocking, Hawkeye, the Trapper, Pathfinder, and Deerslayer), 22, 28, 32-37, 40, 42-48, 53-54, 78, 80-88, 92-93, 105, 112-13, 147-48, 150, 153-54
Bush, Ishmael, 45-48, 88, 122, 147-48, 150, 153

Chainbearer, The, 13, 121-24, 127, 144, 154
Chingachgook (John Mohegan), 33-34, 43, 45, 81, 85, 88, 105
Chronicles of Cooperstown, The, 160
Coffin, Long Tom, 28, 40, 150
Conrad, Joseph, 20-21, 37, 106, 114; "Youth," 106
Cooperstown, 11-13, 17, 27, 33, 73
Crater, The, 13, 128-31, 140, 143-44, 148, 154

Deerslayer, The, 12, 18, 20, 22, 54, 58, 80, 84-91, 106, 114, 135, 150, 153-54
Deerslayer (*see* Bumppo, Natty)
Deists, 138-39, 149
DeLancey, Bishop, 21
DeLancey, Susan Augusta, 11, 17
Dodge, Steadfast, 75, 77, 79, 83, 120, 148
Dostoevski, Fedor, 42, 86

Effingham, Edward, 19, 74-77, 81, 117, 124, 152

Effingham, Eve, 19, 74-77, 81, 117, 124
Effingham, John, 20, 74-77, 81, 117, 124
Effingham, Oliver, 33, 74
Emich, Count of Hartenburg, 62-64, 87
Episcopal Church, 21, 108, 120, 129, 151

Finance Controversy, 12, 57, 67-68
Frey, Heinrich (Burgomaster of Duerckheim), 62-64, 87

Gardiner, Roswell, 137-39, 149-50, 154
Gleanings in Europe: England, 72
Gleanings in Europe: [France], 72
Gleanings in Europe: Italy, 72
Goldencalf, Thomas, 69, 71, 148
Grossman, James, 21, 30, 50, 64, 69, 72, 75-76, 96, 116-17, 136
Gulliver, 70

Hardinge, Lucy, 20, 107, 109-12
Harper (George Washington), 19, 30-32
Hawkeye (*see* Bumppo, Natty)
Hawthorne, Nathaniel, 20, 42
Headsman, The, 12, 62, 64-67, 147
Heathcote, Mark, 51-52, 154
Heidegger, Captain (The Red Rover), 49, 101, 132
Heidenmauer, The, 12, 62-64, 87, 89
History of the Navy of the United States of America, The, 12, 160
Home as Found, 12, 19-20, 54, 58, 73-74, 76-81, 84, 87, 89, 93, 113, 127, 149, 152
Homeward Bound, 12, 19-20, 58, 73-78, 81, 87, 89, 93, 152, 154
Hurry Harry (Harry March), 85-89, 148, 155
Hutter, Hetty, 84-87, 154

Hutter, Judith, 20, 85, 87
Hutter, Tom, 84-89, 148, 155

Jack Tier, 13, 131-34, 136-38, 144
James, Henry, 20, 74
Jones, Howard Mumford, 18, 21

Lafayette, 12, 57
"Lake Gun, The," 164
Last of the Mohicans, The, 11, 18-19, 22, 42-46, 51, 81, 88, 114, 153
Leatherstocking tales (*see also The Pioneers, The Last of the Mohicans, The Prairie, The Pathfinder,* and *The Deerslayer*), 26, 28, 42, 45, 48, 51, 54-55, 80-82, 84, 88-89, 91, 113, 145, 147, 153, 156
Leatherstocking (*see* Bumppo, Natty)
"Legends of the Thirteen Republics," 42
Letter to His Countrymen, A, 12, 68
Libel suits, 12, 19, 73
Lincoln, Lionel, 41, 92
Lionel Lincoln, 11, 23, 27, 41-42, 53-54, 91, 97, 105, 155
Littlepage novels (*see also Satanstoe, The Chainbearer,* and *The Redskins*), 13, 18, 93, 116-28, 130-31, 134, 140, 143-45, 147, 156
Littlepage, Corny, 19, 118-21, 130
Littlepage, Hugh, 19, 124-25, 127-28, 130
Littlepage, Mordaunt, 19, 121, 123-24, 130
Lives of Distinguished American Naval Officers, 163
Louis Philippe, 56, 61
Lounsbury, Thomas R., 50, 69
Lutherans, 62-64

Magua, 43-44, 46, 135
Mahtoree, 45-46, 135

Melville, Herman, 37, 113-14
Mercedes of Castile, 12, 23, 80, 155
Methodists, 135
Miles Wallingford, 13, 20, 55, 91-92, 94, 105-6, 109-12, 114-15, 117, 140, 149, 153
Mohegan, John (see Chingachgook)
Monikins, The, 12, 58, 68-72, 87, 89
Mordaunt, Anneke, 20, 118, 121
Munro, Alice and Cora, 19, 43

Ned Myers, 162
Newcome, Jason, 118-21, 123-25, 134, 148
Notions of the Americans, 12, 27, 57, 159

Oakes, Sir Gervaise, 93-97, 147
Oak Openings, The, 13, 131, 135-37, 139, 144, 148, 150, 155
Orwell, George, 70; 1984, 60, 70

Pathfinder, The, 12, 19, 54, 58, 80-84, 88-89, 152-53
Pathfinder (see Bumppo, Natty)
Peter, Scalping, 135-37, 139, 155
Pilot, The, 11, 18, 26-28, 37-41, 54, 75, 92, 148, 154, 156
Pilot, The (John Paul Jones), 28, 38-40, 154
Pioneers, The, 11, 18, 20, 26-28, 32-38, 40, 42-46, 48, 55, 74, 76, 88, 90, 114, 117, 148, 152-53
Prairie, The, 11, 42, 45-49, 52, 55, 81, 84, 98, 122, 138, 149-50, 153
Precaution, 11, 17, 23-26, 113
Protestants (Radical sects), 79, 120, 122-25, 151
Puritans, 50-53

Red Rover, The, 11, 49, 53, 92, 100, 131-33

Red Rover, The (see Heidegger, Captain)
Redskins, The, 13, 115, 124-28, 131, 143, 149, 152, 155
Robinson Crusoe, by Defoe, 128
Roman Catholic Church, 62-63, 93, 97-99, 101

Satanstoe, 13, 20, 22, 117-21, 124, 127, 144, 152
Scott, Sir Walter, The Pirate, 37
Sea Lions, The, 13, 92, 131, 137-40, 144, 149-50, 154
Sketches of Switzerland, 72
Sketches of Switzerland: Part Second, 72
Skimmer of the Seas, 49, 101
Skinners, 29-31, 61, 105
Smollett, Tobias, 32
Spiller, Robert E., 19, 57, 69, 74, 117
Spy, The, 11, 18-19, 21, 24, 26-32, 37-38, 40, 54-55, 61, 80, 90-91, 93, 100, 105, 113, 134, 146, 148-49, 153, 156
Strides, Joel, 102-5, 146

Tales for Fifteen, 158
Temple, Elizabeth, 35, 74
Temple, Judge Marmaduke, 28, 33-37, 47, 76, 88, 117, 140, 147-48, 152, 154, 159, 164
Thousandacres, Aaron, 122-25, 127, 129, 148, 150
Three Mile Point, 12, 73-74, 79
Towns of Manhattan, The, 145
Truck, Captain, 74-75, 154
Twain, Mark, 18, 88
Two Admirals, The, 12, 18, 54, 91-97, 100, 106, 109, 113-14, 146

Uncas, 43, 45-46, 88, 105
Upside Down, 145

Van Rensselaer, Stephen, 115

Wallingford, Miles, 19, 106-13, 118, 128, 133, 150, 152-54

Washington, George (*see also* Harper), 28, 80, 100

Water-Witch, The, 12, 27, 49-50, 53, 56, 100-1, 133

Ways of the Hour, The, 13, 24, 131, 140-45, 149-50, 152

Wept of Wish-ton-Wish, The, 12, 49-55, 105, 112, 114, 135, 150, 154, 156

Wharton, Captain Henry, 29-31, 100

Wharton, Mr., 29, 31, 61, 134, 146, 148

Willoughby, Bob, 101, 104, 113, 146

Willoughby, Captain Hugh, 92-93, 102-4, 108, 110, 113, 146, 153

Wing-and-Wing, The, 12, 92-93, 97-101, 106, 109, 113-14, 149

Winters, Yvor, 20, 50, 72, 86

Wolfe, Reverend Meek, 52-53, 154-55

Woolston, Mark, 128-30, 133, 139, 150, 154

Wyandotté, 12, 18, 54, 91-93, 101-7, 109, 113-14, 134, 146, 149-50, 153

Yale, 11, 17

Yvard, Raoul, 93, 97-101, 104, 106, 149

Zoellner, Robert H., 82

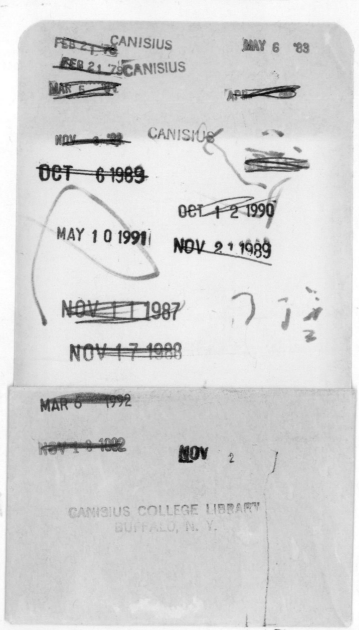